D1601313

Sydney Omarr (left) creator and author of THOUGHT DIAL, shown with Ben Hunter, Los Angeles radio and television personality who was instrumental in helping to make the early editions of this work popular. Note reference to Hunter in chapter on "Picking Winners."

THOUGHT DIAL...

creates a new dimension within the mantic sciences, blending ancient concepts of planet and number symbols with modern, Jungian psychology. The author's presentation of his original research is fresh and creative. Through six previous editions the publishers have been gratified by the enthusiastic reception accorded a book aimed at probing darkened areas of the human mind.

WHAT OTHERS SAY...

Carl Payne Tobey, mathematician: "Sydney Omarr has discovered a method of helping people to contact the abstract world, where all answers to all questions can be found."

Henry Miller, author: "The value of *Thought Dial* lies in the discovery — sooner or later — that all the answers to all questions must come from within. When one becomes truly aware of this ancient truth one will learn to ask the right questions ..."

Ariel Yvon Taylor, Authority on Numbers: Sydney Omarr... more than any writer of the present day, has made clear that Number, like Music, speaks a universal language."

WHAT IT IS...

THOUGHT DIAL is a psychological device which opens new vistas within what Jung terms the "mantic sciences," including astrology and numerology. Invaluable for student as well as professional, it could mark the start of exciting experiences and research — for you! This enlarged, seventh edition contains valuable, new material.

SYDNEY OMARR...

occupies a unique position, having worked to introduce the dynamic element of time in man's continuing search for himself. His name is a by-word among astrologers. His battle against academic prejudice has been ceaseless. His debates, articles, books, radio and television appearances have attracted persons of such diversified interests as science editor John J. O'Neill, mystery writer Craig Rice, novelist Aldous Huxley, writers Henry Miller, William Carlos Williams, Tiffany Thayer, James Boyer May and astrologer-mathematician Carl Payne Tobey, who states flatly: "If Sydney Omarr is unorthodox, then to hell with orthodoxy."

Omarr is the author of *My World of Astrology* and numerous other books, including *Henry Miller: His World of Urania, Dream-Scope, Astrology — Its Role In Your Life, The Truth About Astrology.* His syndicated column on astrology appears in newspapers around the world. Omarr is executive editor of *BORDERLINE,* The Magazine That Dares the Unknown. His approach to so-called "borderline" subjects is marked by the kind of articulation that attracts those who are skeptics as well as "believers."

Omarr is widely-recognized for his knowledge of the mantic sciences, his efforts to popularize underground elements of modern literature, and for his new editing, writing and reporting. He is a thorn in the side of the orthodox and is often the subject, if not the instigator, of intellectual controversy.

THOUGHT DIAL

By SYDNEY OMARR

Introduction
By Carl Payne Tobey

Published by
Melvin Powers
WILSHIRE BOOK COMPANY
12015 Sherman Road
No. Hollywood, California 91605
Telephone: (213) 875-1711 / 983-1105

Printed by
HAL LEIGHTON PRINTING COMPANY
P.O. Box 3952
North Hollywood, California 91605
Telephone: (213) 983-1105

Seventh Edition

First Printing, May, 1958
Second Printing, January, 1959
Third Printing, September, 1959
Fourth Printing, October, 1960
Fifth Printing, March, 1961
Sixth Printing, October, 1962
Seventh Printing, July, 1965

ISBN 0-87980-164-6
PRINTED IN THE UNITED STATES OF AMERICA

*Sydney Omarr will be happy to receive results of your
experiments with the Thought Dial. Address him in care of
9TH HOUSE PUBLISHING CO.
Box 1092, Hollywood, Calif. 90028

CONTENTS

Visiting with Sydney Omarr, to discuss astrology and THOUGHT DIAL, are: (left to right) society columnist Cobina Wright of Hollywood; S. George Little, President of General Features Corporation; Florence Morley, French motion picture star; and Omarr.

Strong Man Mickey Hargitay, Jayne Mansfield and Sydney Omarr — the startled looks are the result of a demonstration of THOUGHT DIAL.

ACKNOWLEDGEMENTS

I would like, first of all, to acknowledge a debt of gratitude, long due, to Carl Payne Tobey, president of the Institute of Abstract Science at Tucson, Arizona. It was Mr. Tobey, a fine mathematician, astrologer and writer, who first encouraged me to continue work on the Thought Dial, who offered the facilities of his organization at Tucson, and who published the first review of this work in his excellent **Student Forum.**

It was many years ago, in New York, that I first encountered Tobey. I w a s t h e n publishing ASTROLOGY NEWS, **The Trade Journal of Astrology.** It was the first such publication in the field. Like all firsts, it was not always easy going. Among those who supported the young man brash enough to step in where older, wiser heads feared to tread, were Carl Payne Tobey—and the founder of the publishing house issuing this present work: Llewellyn George.

The late Mr. George was one of the finest gentlemen to be found anywhere, in or out of astrology. And there were others who foresaw the need of a journalistic approach in covering the vast field of astrology: persons and individuals who lent moral and financial support. Though ASTROLOGY NEWS no longer is issued, its influence is still being felt in modern astrology, where today it is no longer unusual for publications to report in a concise, objective manner, on what astrologers are writing, doing and thinking, and also what the field, in general, is doing to better its sorely neglected concept of public relations.

As I say, there were a number of persons and organizations, through their initial support of the trade paper, who can claim credit for this healthy trend. Ralph Schaeffer of New York, was one. The Church of Light in Los Angeles, was another. Dorothea and Robert DeLuce, also of Los Angeles, were most enthusiastic, and in the same city The Self-Realization Fellowship was a regular advertiser. The individuals who came forward to be counted make up a who's who of astrology, including Nona Howard of Boston; Blanca Holmes of Los Angeles; Ernest Grant of Washington, D.C.; Charles Luntz of St. Louis; Edward Wagner of New York; and the list could be extended, including Marc Edmund Jones, the late Elbert Benjamine, Doris Chase Doane, and on and on to Florence Campbell, Clifford Cheasley, etc.

All this, perhaps, has nothing to do with the Thought Dial. Not on the surface, anyway. But the experience, with ASTROLOGY NEWS, convinced me that those who engage in the study of astrology are practicing a universal language, one which is destined, as it was in the past, to be spoken with greater regularity.

It was Tobey, with his knowledge of mathematics, who was able to comprehend the **idea of thoughts through numbers.** He was sure that the Thought Dial represented a valuable contribution **to workers** both in the fields of psychology and astrology. His enthusiasm has never wavered.

Like Tobey, I feel we have, in the Thought Dial, a key to a better understanding of numerical and planetary symbols. And, through these symbols, an added key to the mysteries of the subconscious mind. I believe that the subconscious, just as it does in dreams, attempts to make itself heard via these symbols.

I have earned somewhat of a reputation for reliability in the fields of news and astrology. It is a reputation I value. I gladly stake it on the Thought Dial.

—Sydney Omarr
Los Angeles, California
February, 1958

INTRODUCTION

by Carl Payne Tobey

President, Institute of Abstract Science

In order to explain the Thought Dial, it would be necessary to explain the mind, and no one has done a very good job of that up till now. Explanations have been attempted by theologists, philosophers, psychiatrists and metaphysicians, but none of these explanations have been very ingenious. Educators regard it as a vacuum into which you pour something. Biologists think it is a bunch of cells in the brain. Freud placed it nearer the sex organs.

Because educators look upon the mind as a vacuum into which you pour something, it is seldom realized that all truth had to originally come out of the mind of someone. The greatest truths are abstract truths. When we point to an object and say it is a tree, this does not involve any kind of truth. It has merely to do with man's idiotic habit of classifying everything into groups. The great abstract truths are mathematical truths, theorems, etc. All of man's progress and all real science is based on such abstract truths. These truths came out of the minds of men. Truth is something that exists in an abstract form, and were it not possible for us to contact it, there would be no known mathematical theorems. Without these, there could be no science. The only true science is mathematics. It is pure abstraction. Other so-called sciences are largely hoaxes, for they are merely a matter of classifying things according to some predetermined arrangement.

Mathematical truths are discovered when they come into the mind of someone. The history of mathematics shows that mathematicians often awaken out of sleep with some great truth in their minds, or they dream a mathematical theorem. It comes to them in a dream. Churches, schools, colleges and universities leave us with the impression that truths are found in textbooks. When statistical principles were first employed to prove the existence of extra-sensory perception, precognition, clairvoyance, etc., John J. O'Neill, late science editor of the **New York Herald Tribune,** wrote that science had just discovered what everybody had always known.

Words like "clairvoyance" were in the dictionary long before science ever investigated them. Folks talked about second sight, but over a long interval anyone able to bring forth truth from the abstract in such a manner was regarded as a witch and an agent of the devil. Churches and other social institutions had various methods of dealing with witches. In the western desert part of our own country, where water is scarce and water dowsers are relied upon by ranchers and banks, the term "water witch" is still prevalent.

It was not too long ago that only women believed in intuition. The first statistical tests conducted by Dr. J. B. Rhine of Duke University demonstrated that one out of five persons, on the average, has some degree of extra-sensory perception. One of the principal reasons why the other four do not have it is because they have been **taught** not to have it by our odd educational system. They have been taught that there is no such factor. They have been taught to ignore their intuition and their hunches and stick to the doctrine of materialism. Of course, this has been changing since the 1929 crash in the stock market when a relatively small portion of the public began to **question** our authorities.

Back in 1938, the writer was one of the persons

who took the extra-sensory perception tests at Duke University, as given by the late Dr. Charles Stuart, mathematician and expert in this field at that time. The writer proved to. be one of those four who showed no signs of extra-sensory perception. He left Duke with several decks of the extra-sensory perception test cards, and headed to Florida, where he began making tests on many people. He made a few observations of his own. He noted that his **best** subjects were people born during the interval of each year when the Sun is in Sagittarius. He noted that people who could not score above normal usually guessed the **first card correctly.** This factor was later investigated at Duke, with similar results. He also noted that, in his own case, when there were but five symbols to guess from, he could picture all five symbols at once. This seemed a handicap. With others, he observed that relaxation of a subject had much to do with correct guessing. He conducted an experiment of his own with himself as a subject.

He used an ordinary deck of playing cards, 52 in number, where he had to guess a specific card with the odds 51 to 1 against him. After the cards were carefully shuffled and cut, they were put away on a secluded table, until sometime within the next 24 hours, when the writer had an involuntary impression of a card from the deck. When this happened, the card was written down, and then checked against the top card on the deck. He succeeded in guessing the first five cards correctly. If this was due to chance, it was against odds of 380,204,031 to 1.

In later years, he tried using such faculties for discovering mathematical formulas. He discovered the prime number **dendrite,** which mathematicians had sought unsuccessfully for 2500 years. All he did was relax and reflect on the problem after retiring in bed at night. On the third night, he had the answer.

The writer is convinced that actually **all knowledge** of any subject is within your own mind at all times, because it is there in the **abstract**. The problem is to bring it forth. There is an abstract world. You have contact with that world if you wish to exercise it. In the abstract world, there is no time and no space. You can only have time when there is change. Nothing ever changes in the abstract world. Any mathematical theorem is the same today as it was in the time of Euclid and Pythagoras in 500 B.C. The great mathematicians, who have been the greatest of all scientists, have been men who were able to contact the abstract world. You need have no insecurity when dealing with the abstract world because you need never fear that anything in it will ever change. The whole study of the abstract world comes under the heading of mathematics. Mathematics deals only with the abstract. Its application in the material world is something else again. Even astrology is actually a study of the abstract, and therefore, is a form of mathematics. Perhaps the best branch of mathematics to study, to learn to see what the abstract world is like, is **Number Theory,** originally given birth by a mathematician named Fermat. In 500 B.C., Pythagoras was seeking something similar in **numerology.** Perhaps Fermat was one of our best examples of a man who was able to contact the abstract world and write down what he saw there. He discovered a vast number of new mathematical theorems.

The abstract world is a world of design. It is beautiful design. All great mathematicians have seen the abstract world as a world of beauty and have described it as such. Our educators do not teach us to see into the abstract world. They merely teach us to memorize what others have recorded from that world, or to know where to look it up in a book of formulas. When you can do this, you are not necessarily a mathematician, but you may be an engineer. Engineers apply the mathematical knowledge that others have brought back from the abstract world.

A true conception of the word "intellect" would involve that part of the mind with which we may contact the abstract world. **We stand in a balance between the intellectual and the emotional worlds.** The emotions have their own purposes, but they cut us off from the abstract and prevent our use of the intellect. To contact the abstract, we have to walk away from the emotional. You almost have to be alone to contact the abstract through the intellect. Society is an emotional organism. When you follow society, you have little chance of contacting the abstract. You have to cut yourself away from society. You contact the abstract best when you learn to be alone, completely independent and immune to what others may think about anything. Even our religions belong mainly to the emotional rather than to the intellectual world. There is no devil in the abstract world. He is a product of the imagination we find in the emotional religious world. Yet, when the theologist speaks of the Will of God, he is seeking the abstract world, for the abstract world is the Will of God. It is the Word.

The laws that govern the universe are abstract laws. Physical laws are actually abstract, although material obeys them. Sir Isaac Newton, who discovered the laws of gravitation, saw them not as any force, but as abstract mathematical law. The laws of planetary motion are abstract mathematical laws discovered by an astrologer named Kepler. No astronomers can explain why all free bodies in space travel in ellipses rather than in circles. They just do. They obey a mathematical law.

Now, what is the **Thought Dial** of Sydney Omarr?

When you want to know the correct time, you can dial a number on your telephone and get the right answer, all automatically. In a way, the Thought Dial operates in somewhat the same man-

14

ner. At least, it has for the writer on numerous occasions. It has turned up with the right answers in some manner.

You may have a question on your mind. It may be a very serious question. Probably the more serious the better. You dial a number and zip comes the answer. To say the least, it is remarkable. **It is almost as if you were telephoning some master of all wisdom within yourself.** He sees all and tells all. This is just the writer's reaction to what he has seen, but it would seem that Omarr has devised a means of bypassing the conscious and getting into the unconscious. I won't say the subconscious, because I think it may involve the superconscious. I think the superconscious mind contains a super calculating device that makes all electronic calculators look like simplicity itself. I know there is such a device because I have often employed it in mathematical work. I too have awakened in the night with the answer to a very complicated mathematical problem clearly before me. This takes practice and relaxation, but Omarr seems to have a means of going to less trouble. He appears to bypass the conscious in the same or a similar manner to that in which the conscious is bypassed in hypnotism. The function may not be too unlike the individual who prays for divine guidance and gets it. There are many people who do not believe this can be accomplished, never try it and never get divine guidance. Perhaps the Thought Dial is a means of getting divine guidance.

If the Thought Dial is unorthodox, then to hell with orthodoxy. We have been taught enough claptrap by orthodoxy. You can never be an intellectual until you toss orthodoxy and all of its superstitions out of the window. Much that has been taught as science is pure superstition. A large part of astronomy is mere superstition. A large part of what has been taught as religion is superstition. We will meet the true science and the true religion as one and the

15

same thing in the abstract mathematical world. The Thought Dial deals with numbers. Frankly, I do not know whether it has has anything to do with numbers and their actual characteristics as studied in Number Theory, or whether the numbers actually apply only as a part of some code between the conscious and the unconscious. I do know that numbers have characteristics and that no two numbers have exactly the same characteristics. Anyone who understands Number Theory knows that. Numbers are all a part of that great cosmic and abstract design, and everything that ever happens in the universe happens only in accord with the abstract design.

Perhaps the Thought Dial is a means of contacting the abstract.

It seems appropriate that the Thought Dial should be published in a year when men are re-examining their moth-eaten educational system in order to see what changes are going to be necessary in the era of space travel that is approaching. You can use the Thought Dial as something that is entertaining, or you can take it more seriously. Perhaps it will set you to thinking. Perhaps it will help you to learn more about the human mind— your mind. Perhaps it will help to open up some of the unlimited possibilities of mind that have been hidden from us by so much false science and so much false religion. Try it out. See what it does for you.

People often joke about looking into a crystal ball to see what the future holds. They joke about it, because they can't see what the future would be doing in a crystal ball. It isn't there. The crystal is merely a means to an end. It is a means of fixing the conscious attention on a point and allowing the unconscious to take over. In this way, some form of contact with the abstract appears to take place for some people. You might be able to see nothing in a crystal ball. Most people couldn't. A materialist could smash a crystal to bits and prove to his own satisfaction that there is no future in a crystal ball, but materialists have never heard of that factor we call mind. They cannot deal nor cope with what they do not know exists.

The views expressed here are the writer's own. Insofar as Sydney Omarr's views are concerned, he is about to tell them to you himself. Read what he has to say. Meanwhile, happy dialing.

PRINCIPLES

The Thought Dial, though it can be utilized for fun and amusement, is more, much more than a toy. It is an instrument based on sound, psychological principles, especially those put forth by the renowned psychologist, Dr. Carl G. Jung of Zurich, Switzerland.

In his work, **The Interpretation of Nature and the Psyche,** * Dr. Jung uses the word, "synchronicity," and explains it thusly: . . . "simultaneous occurrence of a certain psychic state with one or more external events which appear as meaningful parallels to the momentary subjective state—and, in certain cases, vice versa."

Dr. Jung makes use of the term to depict a coincidence in time of two or more events. It should be pointed out that he makes no claim that the events are causally related. In fact, he defines synchronicity as the simultaneous occurrence of two meaningfully but **not** causally connected events.

Students of astrology should find this easy to comprehend, especially those who have studied the writings of Carl Payne Tobey of Tucson, Arizona. Tobey stresses that events which appear to coincide with planetary positions and aspects are **not** representative of causal phenomena. Rather, says Tobey, astrology is a form of abstract, mathematical expression.

Perhaps the Thought Dial can best be compared to horary astrology, in which a question, thought or idea is presumed to be "born" and a chart is set up

*Pantheon Books, New York (1955)

for the moment of birth, as if the question, thought or idea was a human being for whom a horoscope was being cast.

The Thought Dial represents, in one sense, **horary astrology with numbers.**

The Thought Dial is the utilization of Jung's principle of synchronicity, in that a thought, a question or idea, is reduced or defined, at a certain time, into a number and planetary symbol.

The Thought Dial is a valid, **mantic** procedure for tapping the subconscious: thoughts, like everything else in nature, find expression through numbers. As Pythagoras said, "Nature geometrizes!"

Jung declares: "Since the remotest times men have used numbers to express meaningful coincidences . . . those that can be interpreted."

Dr. Jung is conceded by many to be the greatest living psychologist. He is certainly the biggest "name" psychologist since Freud. Perhaps that is why he has displayed far more courage and originality than his colleagues. He has overcome fear of academic prejudice. He is not afraid to speak out on such subjects as extra-sensory perception, the mystery of numbers, astrology and psychic phenomena. His work and findings lend support to the principles behind the Thought Dial. Jung's studies conclude that numbers and planets, utilized as a method of analyzing character, perceiving thoughts, and foretelling the future—work! So the Thought Dial works. Why it works is of no particular concern here. That is a job for psychologists, other scientists and students to tackle.

Many scientists go along with Jung. However, not having his reputation, they are shy about expressing themselves in public. That is why Jung is mentioned repeatedly here as a reference. But students who are familiar with my previous works know very well that a number of outstanding thinkers have long been intrigued with the vast possibilities such a study as this represents. Jung asserts that a sequence of numbers . . . is more than a mere stringing together of identical units: he says that numbers and synchronicity (a correspondence between an event, thought, etc. and numbers) have always been brought into connection with one another. **Mystery** is a common characteristic of both.

Number, perhaps more than anything else, brings order out of apparent chaos.

To quote Jung again: "It (number) is the predestined instrument for creating order, or for apprehending an already existing, but still unknown, regular arrangement . . ."

He says, too, that number perhaps is the most primitive element of order in the **human mind** . . ."* Jung goes on to declare, "Hence it is not such an audacious conclusion after all if we define number psychologically as an **archetype of order** which has become conscious."

Now, upon first examination or experimentation with the Thought Dial, a natural objection might arise: "But, after all, I don't know what the numbers mean! So how can my conscious or subconscious mind express itself through numerical symbols?"

Once more, let us turn to Jung. He presents the possibility that numbers were **not,** as is commonly thought, invented by man. He emphasizes that numbers are not inventions of the conscious mind. Instead, they are **spontaneous** productions of the unconscious. Jung asserts that ". . . it follows irrefutably that the unconscious uses number as an ordering factor."

Jung stresses, over and again, the possibility that numbers, instead of being products of invention, were **found or discovered.** If this is so, and Jung is

*Boldface mine.

inclined to believe it is, numbers would have the characteristic or quality of being, in Jung's words, **pre-existent to consciousness.**

It can be presumed, at least as a working theory, that the subconscious is familiar with the number-symbols and what they represent. The unconscious mind, or the subconscious, or the super-conscious, races past the conscious, or the **censor,** in expressing itself via these symbols.

Tradition, experimentation and experience are the components making up the number interpretations. Experience, for example, has taught that the number 6 represents domesticity, concern with matters affecting the home: often a change of residence

coincides with subconscious expression totaling 6. That digit is (via the same components) associated with the planet symbol of Venus, which in its turn, represents a zodiacal symbol and area associated with various aspects of character, thought and events.

The subconscious or hidden mind, presumed to be familiar with these symbols and their associations, brings them forth to the conscious area through utilization of the Thought Dial.

Basically, therefore, the Thought Dial operates on ancient and modern concepts of astrology and numerology—and it extends these into the modern field of psychology, being as valid in its way as any other psychological testing device.

To once more quote Dr. Jung, who declares that "Astrology represents the summation of all the psychological knowledge of antiquity."

Astrology is, like everything else, closely associated with number. The Thought Dial, combining number and planet symbols, by-passes the conscious, "censor" mind and probes deep, shaking hands with the truth that inhabits us all.

WHAT THE NUMBERS SYMBOLIZE

Number ONE: This is the start, the beginning: it is birth and life, independence of both thought and action. It is a time for the new, for the launching of projects. This digit is associated with the Sun.

Number TWO: This is a force which is emotional and negative rather than direct and positive. It is symbolic of diplomacy. It is a time for winning ways, for tact. This is a caution mark, wait and see. The number is associated with the Moon.

Number THREE: This number represents a relief of pressure: it is symbolic of humor and versatility. It is a time for getting out of a rut. However, a scattering of forces must be avoided. The temptation is to try doing too much at one time. The number is associated with Jupiter.

Number FOUR: This is the square: it is routine and hard work and the handling of details. There is strength here, but only if creative thought or imagination is brought into play. This is a time to slow down. The number is associated with Uranus.

Number FIVE: Change and travel, the creative arts, relations with members of the opposite sex, speculation—these are stressed. Communication of ideas becomes a necessity. Personal magnetism is heightened. The digit is associated with the planet Mercury.

Number SIX: Emphasis is on the home, change of residence, the rediscovering of loved ones. Diplomacy is a requirement here, just as with the number 2, only in a larger sense. Stress definitely is on the home. The digit is associated with Venus.

Number SEVEN: The keyword is self-deception: the tendency is to see persons and situations as they might ideally be, instead of the way they actually exist. Not a time to enter into legal pacts. An aura of illusion dominates. The number is associated with the planet Neptune.

Number EIGHT: Power, strength, finances, reproduction, marriage, stress on business affairs—these represent the symbols of this number. It is a time for pushing ahead—hard. No time for a slowdown here. The number is associated with Saturn.

Number NINE: This is completion, the end of a cycle: a time to finish projects. Avoid new starts, be wary of new contacts at this period. Often indicates the bearing of another's responsibility. Universal appeal, wide publicity also shown. The number is associated with Mars.

Number ELEVEN: A higher octave of 2. A master digit. Stress is on intuition, teaching. Hunches are to be trusted here. The influence is far-reaching; it is a time for expressing ideas, no matter how radical. The number is associated with Uranus.

Number TWENTY-TWO. A higher octave of 4. A master digit. Emphasis is on building, creating, making master plans. Must not be bogged down with detail or influenced by persons with no vision. The number is associated with the planet Pluto.

NUMBERS AS OBJECTS

It was the late writer Gertrude Stein who, perhaps more than any other person in modern times, treated words as "objects." She felt that each word was an entity in itself; she became fascinated with words for the life within them, for the "vibrations" or meanings expressed. Miss Stein, sometimes, became so enamored with the words as **separate** objects that she deliberately overlooked meanings as a **whole.** She was, in this sense, a writer's writer. The general reading public, though at times they could sense what she was talking or writing about, most often found her outrageously funny. But her influence has prevailed. Her mark is to be found in some of the best of modern works. In effect, she was the conductor of a noble experiment—she had taken hold of the language and was shaking it violently, shaking some life back into the English language. And while the general public laughed at her "words as objects," the persons she influenced were forever in her debt, and were being celebrated by the same public that found it fashionable to smirk at Gertrude Stein, the mentor of such as Ernest Hemingway, Thornton Wilder, Sherwood Anderson, Richard Wright and others.

Miss Stein had conducted numerous experiments in so-called automatic writing, under the tutorship of the famed philosopher William James. Words had become objects, similar to numbers, often **denoted** by number.

All this is by way of introducing the notion of numbers as objects, as forces or influences: the number 1, for example, standing as a beacon to the new, to independence, to originality, to exploration of uncharted courses. Number 1, like all numbers, is one thing as a **symbol,** and quite another when taken alone as a number, or utilitarian object to be part of the operation involved in adding or subtracting, multiplying or dividing, etc.

In this sense, mathematicians and numerologists are much closer to agreement than are astronomers and astrologers. Astronomers, on the whole, are stuck with the idea that planets are to be measured only for position and size; as far as **influences** are concerned, or planets as symbols, astronomers remain woefully ignorant, or stubborn, or both.

With mathematicians, the story is different. **Mathematicians are more familiar with numbers than astronomers are with planets.**

This fact becomes obvious after only the most superficial examination. I, for one, can testify to the obstinacy of astronomers. I have debated with at least three leading astronomers on the subject of astrology. The astronomers claimed, before the debates, to know the subject of astrology. After the debates, however, each admitted he had little or no knowledge of the subject. Why, then, did they debate in the first place? That question, in itself, would require a separate study, a psychological one. The astronomers, generally, have a fixed, **erroneous** concept of astrology. When their views are exposed to the light of public debate, this fact is forcibly driven home.

It was the late Pulitzer Prize winner, John J. O'Neil, science editor of the **New York Herald-Tribune,** who wrote me, after my debate with Dr. Roy K. Marshal,* that such attacks on astrology must, from now on, be regarded as symptoms of professional paranoia.

These incidents are related here because astrology, or the symbols utilized in the subject, combine

*Former director of Fels Planetarium in Philadelphia.

with numbers to make the Thought Dial an instrument of value.

Number 1, through tradition and experiment, is associated with the Sun, which in turn is related to the zodiacal sign of Leo the Lion. So, the digit, although it denotes independence, also is related to thoughts, things and events associated with the Sun and with Leo. Taking Aries as the natural first sign of the zodiac, Leo becomes the fifth sign or house, associated with affairs of the heart, speculation, adventure, children. Leo rules the heart and back and is strongly connected, also, with entertainment and with forces that are creative, from sex to artistic expression. Leo is the showman, as the most elementary student of the zodiac can testify.

Now, there are a number of systems of house division in astrology. The one being used in this work is a traditional one, the one which associates Leo with the fifth house. **But it is not the only one.** Mr. Tobey, in his brilliant, original researches, places Leo at the forefront, as related to the first house. His work has added much to astrology, has often turned the subject inside-out, emptying it of numerous false notions. But the vast majority of experiments conducted with the Thought Dial involved the so-called traditional method, making Aries the natural first house indicator, Taurus the second, Gemini the third, Cancer the fourth, Leo the fifth, and so on down the line, to Pisces as the twelfth house.

It is my belief that, through further experiments, a combination of the Tobey system and the traditional one, as used here, will prove of immense value. For example, in the Tobey system, Leo is a first house sign. Leo is associated with the Sun in both methods. And, though Leo is traditionally a fifth house sign, the Sun is associated with number 1, the FIRST digit, the beginning, the pioneer, the start, self-expression, etc.

Leo, though traditionally of fifth house value, most certainly contains elements of the FIRST, also. The same is true of Cancer. In traditional methods, Cancer is the fourth house. Tobey places that sign on the cusp of the second house of the natural zodiac. The Moon, which rules Cancer, is number 2. So, **through numbers,** the similarities become more evident than the differences!

The student will soon become aware, as I have pointed out to Tobey and other leading astrologers and number students, that the **house meanings themselves** are too similar to the number symbols for this to be mere coincidence. It is my belief that the astrological houses gained their meanings **from the numbers.**

Creative mathematicians are in agreement that numbers indeed are objects containing properties of their own, meanings, symbols, "personalities," even influences of their own. Without number, there wouldn't be very much of anything else, certainly not much of a civilization as we know it today.

As Constance Reid points out, in her excellent book, **From Zero to Infinity,*** "number is an abstraction, a recognition of the fact that collections may have something in common even though the elements of the collection have in common nothing whatsoever." Or, as Bertrand Russell declared, "It must have required many ages to discover that a brace of pheasants and a couple of days were both instances of the number 2." In other words, numbers are objects in themselves, to be studied for individual meanings and properties, and numbers, also, are abstractions, representing, among other things, **symbols of thoughts or ideas.**

This, perhaps, becomes easier to comprehend when we think of words as symbols of our thoughts. It is not only **not** fantastic to think of words as depicting our thoughts, or expressing them, it would

*Thomas Y. Crowell Company, New York (1955)

be ridiculous to deny that power to words. Words, thus, are related to numbers, **once the numbers are understood.** Words, through numbers, are easier to understand, as a study of the works of Cheiro, or Ariel Yvonne Taylor, or Florence Campbell, or Clifford Cheasley or other numerologists will reveal. Words, through a simple process, can be transformed to number, each letter containing a numerical value of its own, just as each number contains a letter value, an element (number 4 is an "earth element"), a characteristic, a thought symbol, etc.

Numbers are the objects upon which the Thought Dial is built and upon which, to a large extent, it operates.

Thoughts are abstract expressions made solid (objects) and thus easier to examine and comprehend—through the use of numbers.

The Thought Dial helps makes this possible.

HOW TO OPERATE THE THOUGHT DIAL

Operation of the Thought Dial is simple—that is, as far as the physical movements or operations are concerned. In this sense, a finger, preferably the forefinger, is placed on the arrow, as indicated. And the arrow is moved to three digits, which are then added and reduced to a single number. **The only double numbers retained as totals are 11 and 22.** That is the simple part.

But there is more to the Thought Dial than the mere physical apparatus, or "going through the motions."

It is important to form a thought clearly, concisely: either in the form of a question, a picture-thought, or through the simple act of relaxing, so your number selections are not hurried. In many cases, the arrow **will move** fast, so fast it will appear to be moving itself. In other instances, the process may resemble a man confined to a torture chamber—everything slow, crawling, nothing definite. When finally you have dialed three numbers, perspiration will stand out on your forehead. Other times, all will be harmony. The arrow indicates three numbers and the total is arrived at—the interpretation given, an answer or solution found. **Actions of the Thought Dial depend upon your state of mind, your thoughts or your questions.**

Remember, the Thought Dial is merely a physical instrument through which you measure and analyze intangibles, such as thoughts, questions, ideas, speculation about the future. The Thought Dial, in your hands, is basically YOU!

Now, let us confine ourselves to the physical operation of the Thought Dial.

First, place the forefinger on the arrow, as indicated. Then, after your thought, idea, or question is formed, or when you are simply relaxed, allow your finger, or the arrow **to carry your finger,** to any three numerical symbols. The start, of course, is made where indicated, from the zero symbol.

The three numbers are then added and reduced to a single digit. The only double numbers retained are 11 and 22.

Suppose, for example, you dial 4 . . . 8 . . . and 6. These numbers total 4 plus 8 plus 6 = 18.

Number 18 is reduced to a single number by adding from left to right, thus: 1 plus 8 = 9. The Thought Dial total of 4 plus 8 plus 6 is 9.

It is a simple operation. Number 9, in this instance, becomes the symbol of your subconscious thought, or question, or idea—it tells something of the character of your mind or thoughts at the moment, and tells much more, too.

The interpretations are given in the various sections of this book: YOUR SUBCONSCIOUS THOUGHTS, HOW TO LOCATE LOST ARTICLES, YOUR QUESTIONS ANSWERED, THE YES AND NO TECHNIQUE, AND PICKING WINNERS.

But always check the number symbols, so that you become familiar with them, so that you can experiment. Take notes, test the Thought Dial. Let us have your findings.

For example, in this case the total is 9. A check of the section **What the Numbers Symbolize** tells us that number 9 is associated with completion, the end of a cycle. It is a time to finish projects rather than to try new projects. Number 9, it has been found, often is the nurse, the humanitarian: it is a person, too, who carries another's load on his shoulders. It is time to discard the past, to get rid of burdens—to prepare for the future.

Generally, as an indicator of SUBCONSCIOUS THOUGHTS, the number 9 would indicate that one phase of life or activity was drawing to a close, a new one about to begin.

Number 9, in answer to a DIRECT QUESTION, would answer that this was the end of an association, a relationship, a project—the answer would be in terminating a relationship and getting ready to start out with new ideas—a display of independence.

As a symbol for LOCATING LOST OBJECTS, number 9—literally—might mean that a child has the object among some clothing.

In the YES AND NO technique, number 9 would be considered positive, or YES.

In PICKING WINNERS, number 9 would be associated with Mars, and with names of horses or teams or athletes whose names were similar to Mars-9 relationships, such as: IRON, COMPLE-TION, ACTION, FIGHTER, WAR LORD, LEADER, INVENTOR, etc.

Each section, of course, contains complete explanations and interpretations.

For now, let us review the basic operation:

1. Relax. Form thought or question clearly in mind.
2. Place forefinger on indicator, which rests at zero position.
3. Continue to concentrate.
4. Move dial, or allow it to move, to any three digits.
5. Total the three numbers.

6. Reduce all double numbers, with the exception of 11 and 22, by adding from left to right.

7. The total is your Thought Dial indicator, the symbol of that particular thought, idea, or question.

NOTE: Dial **any** three numbers, using zero position as a starting point. This does **not** eliminate zero as a number. For example, you could dial 3 . . . 0 . . . 7, which would total 10. When added, 10 would equal 1 plus zero, or 1.

If your total should be zero, which would result if you dialed to zero three times, then you should once more relax, concentrate upon your thought, and start over.

You CAN repeat numbers. For example, you could dial 7 . . . 6 . . . 7.

Allow yourself FREEDOM OF THOUGHT, or motion. You can dial around the circle or not, as you wish or **think.**

That is the physical operation of the Thought Dial. From here on, we will be most concerned with INTERPRETATIONS of totals which result from this operation.

EXAMPLE: Subject dials numbers 22, 8 and 11. These numbers are added:

22 plus 8 plus 11 = 41.

4 plus 1 = 5.

The total of 22, 8 and 11 equals 5.

REPEATING: The only double numbers kept as final totals are 11 and 22! All other numbers are reduced to single digits by adding from left to right.

NUMBERS AND THOUGHTS

It is a known fact that, prior to his death, inventor Thomas Alva Edison was hard at work on a so-called "Telephone Between Worlds," an instrument through which, Edison hoped, it would be possible to "tune in" or connect with another world, if there be one—the world of the soul, or personality, or memory, or whatever part of man survived after his bodily death. Whether Edison's device involved numbers, or was in any way similar to the Thought Dial, is not known. This is pointed out to show that wise men—men who have pioneered and invented—men like Sir William Crookes, Sir Arthur Conan Doyle, Jung, Edison, and others like them—have not been afraid to experiment with the abstract. Men like Rhine have, in effect, "measured thoughts," often doing so in the face of ridicule from colleagues. It is now, of course, possible to measure brain waves. And it is hoped that the Thought Dial will represent at least a start in the direction of "solidifying" thoughts, ideas, mental impulses, insights into the future, etc.

The validity of the Thought Dial, to a large extent, depends upon numbers as symbols—symbols whose meanings are clear to the subconscious mind, or **continuous memory.**

In his work **The Soul of the Universe,*** scientist-astronomer Dr. Gustaf Stromberg declares that the results of his studies are, "that the individual memory is probably indestructible . . ."

Dr. Stromberg, now of Pasadena, California, came to the United States from Sweden in 1916.

*David McKay Company, New York (1941)

33

He was on the scientific research staff of the Mount Wilson Observatory of the Carnegie Institution of Washington from 1917 to 1946. And of his works, Albert Einstein said, "Very few men could of their own knowledge present . . . material as clearly and concisely as he has succeeded in doing."

And it is Dr. Stromberg who asserts: "The memory of an individual is written in indelible script in space and time—it has become an eternal part of a Cosmos in development." Stromberg is of the opinion that the brain receives **waves** from a kind of universal brain, or soul. That, in effect, the brain is merely a filtering mechanism, permitting certain ideas and thoughts to flow through from "the soul of the universe."

Of **thoughts**, he says . . . "In addition to conscious reasoning there exists also a certain type of unconscious reasoning in which people think with their 'feelings', and sometimes even to better advantage." Stromberg has always been cooperative whenever I have consulted him. I once arranged for a radio discussion between Stromberg, novelist Aldous Huxley, and James Crenshaw, a newspaperman and authority on psychic phenomena. The discussion was of great importance, both for what was said on the air, and statements made "off the record."

One thing Stromberg is "on the record" with is this statement, " . . . thoughts can be transmitted from one individual to another (telepathy), and there is then no logical reason why they cannot be transmitted from an individual to the Soul of the Universe and from the Soul of the Universe to an individual (inspiration)."

This becomes simpler to comprehend when we conceive of the thoughts as symbols, expressed through number. And that, it may be said, is the purpose of the Thought Dial, the combining of numbers and thoughts, the identifying of thoughts and ideas with number symbols.

Now, let us put the Thought Dial to use. It can be used personally, for the solution of your own problems. But the professional psychologist, astrologer or student, as well as the hobbyist, can also utilize the Thought Dial in aiding others.

With experience, other uses will be found; but for now the basic sections which follow are headed:

SUBCONSCIOUS THOUGHTS
DIRECT QUESTIONS ANSWERED
YES AND NO TECHNIQUE
LOCATING LOST ARTICLES
PICKING WINNERS

These "other uses" are references to the skill which practice brings. For example, the subject thinks of an individual, dials three numbers. You total the digits and reduce to a single number. Le us suppose it is 7. That number is associated with the planet Neptune, which rules Pisces. You can start out, thus, by stating that the person being "thought about" was born under Pisces, which would be from February 20 to March 21. And the description of the person would fit the Pisces-Neptune-7 characteristics, and so on. And, often, when a person merely dials three numbers, without necessarily concentrating on a problem, he reveals **his own date of birth.** He does this in the manner provided by the above example.

Experience through experiment will unlock the door to other fascinating procedures and possibilities.

SUBCONSCIOUS THOUGHTS

In this operation, the subject merely dials three numbers, without consciously thinking of a specific question. The idea is to permit the subconscious to come through, past the censor or conscious mind, as it would through a dream. The "dream," in this instance, is the Thought Dial and the number totals.

Remember, in all instances, the subject dials to three numbers, which are added from left to right and reduced to a single number, the only double numbers retained being 11 and 22.

IF THE TOTAL IS ONE:

This number is the individual, the original; it is a need and subconscious desire for independence of thought and action. Originality is stressed. THE SUBJECT HAS A DESIRE TO GIVE OF HIMSELF THROUGH CREATIVE, ORIGINAL, INDIVIDUAL MEANS.

Number 1 is associated with the Sun, which in turn, rules Leo, the natural fifth zodiacal house. The creative urge here is strong, but not necessarily —in this case—as a need for sex expression. Rather, the subject seeks **new forms of expression,** an original way of presenting an old package.

The old is to be discarded in favor of the new, in favor of the pioneer. The subject is being told by his subconscious: TAKE A CHANCE!

The number 1, as a total on the Thought Dial here, represents new enterprises, a chance to get in on the ground floor, to start from the bottom. It represents a need for courage. A pioneer must work and move in the face of obstacles, the biggest obstacle being the past and so-called tried and true methods.

Most often, with this total representing subconscious thought, the subject is perplexed about whether to go along the same path, or take a sharp turn to a new road. THE ANSWER IS THE NEW!

The Sun (symbol of this digit) will attract attention, but its very brightness draws moths—the human kind who damn with faint praise.

Right now, with the 1 total, the subject has no need for the advice of the stable, well-meaning friends and associates. Number 1 is the Sun with a touch of Uranus, just as 4 is Uranus with a touch of the Sun.

SPECULATE! ACT! CREATE!

Members of the opposite sex, because of the Leo-Fifth House influence, often represent a barrier here. So do children, responsibilities, etc.

The element here is FIRE. ORIGINATE, LEAD, PUSH THROUGH PROGRESSIVE MEASURES.

Promote yourself! Your subconscious, in effect, pleads with you to be vain, if necessary, but move AHEAD. On your own!

IF THE TOTAL IS TWO:

Number 2 is associated with the Moon: as a subconscious thought indicator it tells a story of brooding, indecision, worry over the possibility of an abrupt change. This number, as a total on the Thought Dial, stresses the need for DIPLOMACY. The subject is advised to WIN HIS WAY—this rather than resorting to methods of force.

Abrupt decisions, the subconscious is trying to say, should be avoided.

The element of this number is Water. Intuition is stressed. But there is a fine line between intuition and a tendency to make something out of nothing, to worry and brood. Number 2, through its association with the Moon, is also related to the zodiacal sign of Cancer. The tendency here is to collect, to be ultra-sensitive concerning security. But the BEST ADVICE appears to be: SIT TIGHT FOR THE MOMENT!

Number 2, like the digit 6, is the moderator, the diplomat. It will be important for the subject to keep out of triangles. Avoid becoming entangled in battles, controversies. Others will try to involve the subject, will bring him their problems. It would be a mistake, at this time, to take sides. That's the message of the subconscious, as relayed through the Thought Dial.

Avoid weighing yourself down with items which eventually will have to be discarded—that's another significant message to the subject whose total adds to 2. Be aware of security, but avoid being miserly.

Number 2, although it may seem a symbol of **inaction,** is really similar to a yellow traffic light signal. Wait, but be ready. Win your way rather than pushing through by force. Be willing to exercise caution and diplomacy, but do not allow yourself to be squeezed out of the picture. Have patience!

The home is emphasized here. Protection; a valuable ally could appear from your actual home, or near your home, or the ally could be the subject's partner.

The tendency here is to look afar, when actually help may be close by.

Where a 1 total urges action, this digit—2—advises a waiting game. Wait—but remain alert!

By all means avoid brooding! Others may try to

encourage quick decisions. But the subject should review the situation: he would have everything to lose, nothing to gain by impulsive action.

Avoiding impulsive action applies to affairs of the heart, conditions in the home, dealings with older persons, with the parent or parents, with the buying or selling of property.

The subject, through the dialing of this total, should be greatly relieved. The key words are, "No news is good news."

IF THE TOTAL IS THREE:

Number 3 is associated with the planet Jupiter; it is a symbol of expansion and humor, as well as good fortune. However, as a total on the Thought Dial, it often relates to confusion. There is a seriousness of purpose which is generally lacking. The tendency, here, is for the subject to try doing too much at one time. Thus, the subconscious is warning against a scattering of forces. "One thing at a time," is the obvious message. Number 3, through Jupiter, is related to the zodiacal sign of Sagittarius, and with ninth house matters, such as long journeys, both physical as well as journeys of the mind, such as philosophy, higher education, etc. It is a number—this 3—of self-improvement, of gaining through a light touch, a sense of fitness or humor.

The element is Fire; as a total, in relation to subconscious thoughts, the digit expresses a joy in living, tells of improved social life, important contacts to be made at parties, gatherings, etc.

Versatility is a keyword here. The subject should not be tied down to any one method, or person, for that matter. There is a tendency, as revealed through the Jupiter symbol, toward extravagance, not only in financial matters, but in affairs of the heart, in the emotions. For example, to overlook details, to forgive others for their errors, no matter how careless. Generous to a fault—that, too, could describe the state of a person whose total is 3.

Number 3, to use an analogy, is like a baseball player coming up to bat: he carries three bats to the plate, swinging them. Finally, he drops all but one, facing the pitcher with a bat that now feels deceptively light. The subject here has recently unburdened himself of a physical or emotional problem, or both, and he is celebrating, if only in his subconscious mind. All this is fine—if taken for what it is, recognized as a psychological device enabling the subject to better face life, just as the batter now is able to face the pitcher, that bat powerful in his grip, yet the feeling one of lightness, flexibility.

THIS IS NOT THE TIME FOR THE SUBJECT TO BECOME TIED DOWN, EITHER IN BUSINESS DEALS OR IN HIS PERSONAL LIFE.

Wait and see. Be cheerful.

Be enthusiastic without being wasteful.

The truth usually shines through here. That's why the subject has dialed to numbers which total 3, giving the Jupiter-Sagittarius, ninth house symbol. Through use of intuition, "higher mind," the subject has caught a three-dimensional glimpse of his own world, his life, the people surrounding him.

As an indicator of subconscious thought, this total tells the subject to look around, to gain, to avoid being anchored down, for social activities are going to be stepped up and contacts are going to be made—and Lady Luck is putting in an appearance.

IF THE TOTAL IS FOUR:

Number 4 is the square, a fact recognized by both mathematicians and numerologists. It is of the

Earth element. It is associated with Uranus, but also contains elements of the Sun. Number 4, thus, is related, to a large extent, to the zodiacal signs of Aquarius and Leo. It is symbolized by restriction, attention to details, plain, old-fashioned hard work.

The subject, whose total is 4, is tempted to pass on the details to others, to skip a step, to move ahead. Uranus pushes for a change, while the Sun tempts toward immediate glory and publicity. BUT THE SUBCONSCIOUS, THROUGH THE THOUGHT DIAL TOTAL, WARNS THAT THE DETAILS CANNOT BE TRUSTED TO OTHERS. Otherwise, the subject will have to retrace his steps, to move back. This is a time of testing and discipline. Determination must be a keyword for the subject. The subconscious, here, is laying stress upon strength, determination, the details, the plans necessary for change and creative action. BUT THAT CHANGE, THAT ACTION, IS FOR THE FUTURE. PERHAPS THE NEAR FUTURE. BUT IT IS NOT FOR NOW!

Number 4 is solid. And as mathematician Constance Reid states, it is one of the first and most permanent ideas in number—that 4 is the earth number. It is a square similar to the "square" or 90-degree aspect in astrology. It is a test of strength. And if the subject recognizes it as such, he can be patient, knowing that quiet planning now, a gathering of strength, a look around at his assets—can be instrumental to success, perhaps even spectacular success in the future. Careless action now, weakness, will surely lead to disappointment, to failure, to loss.

With the 4 total, the subject had better not listen to advice of friends . . . **at this moment.** The tendency is for friends, no matter how well-meaning, to give advice which would be good in the near-future. BUT NOT FOR NOW! Hopes, wishes, aspirations, creative urges—all of these combine to form GIGANTIC TEMPTATION. The subject wants to break away, to be free from confinement (the square)—but, says the Thought Dial (subconscious), he must first make absolutely sure his foundation is SOLID.

Attention to duty is a necessity. Knowledge of limitations is another. This is the time to BUILD for the FUTURE. To build, not to stand atop an incomplete foundation and shout from the rooftop: again, this is a time of TESTING.

Here is another fact, perhaps the most important of all, in considering 4 as a Thought Dial subconscious thought indicator:

BE AWARE OF OTHER THAN MATERIAL VALUES! Be aware of spiritual and moral issues. In plainer, perhaps less metaphysical language, check your relations with the public (public relations), be sure there is imagination and fire, not just earth and concrete, to your plans, projects, dreams, dealings.

Be patient. Check and double-check.

Your day is coming! It's not today, however.

IF THE TOTAL IS FIVE:

Number 5 is associated with the planet Mercury, and with the zodiacal signs of Gemini and Virgo: it is a symbol of investigation, of analysis, of creativity, relations with members of the opposite sex —it is a number and symbol of romance, of probing, of investigation, curiosity and life itself. The subject, dialing this total, is being told (through subconscious symbolism), to take the road leading to CHANGE, TRAVEL, VARIETY.

Number 5 is the digit, the symbol of COMMUNICATION. Now, there is freedom, just as with number 4, there was the square of restriction. The subject, with this total as a subconscious thought indicator, is thinking of change and travel—and this total ENCOURAGES SUCH A COURSE OF ACTION. The important thing is action. This is the time for change, for revision, for creative, progressive thinking. The element here is Air.

Ambition is keynoted—there is no standing still. Movement and rhythm are emphasized. This is the time for a publicity campaign, for writing, communicating, putting across ideas.

Excesses, of course, must be avoided. This total, as a subconscious indicator, tends to encourage lust, pleasure, the giving in to base appetites. A balance must be struck. Otherwise, a romance (for example) could turn into a sordid affair.

It is here, however, that impulsive action is to be encouraged. The subject, dialing this total, should trust first impressions, should be encouraged to make the try, no matter how high the goal. INTEREST IN MEMBERS OR **A MEMBER** OF THE OPPOSITE SEX IS VERY MUCH IN THE PICTURE. Natural attraction is revealed— the overall pattern is good, encouraging.

This is the time for the subject to probe, to INVESTIGATE. New paths are suggested. Certainly, a change is recommended. It is likely that the subject is concerned with romance, the possibility of marriage, or children—or all of these. The answers to speculation concerning these matters is positive, in the affirmative. Emphasis is placed upon greater FREEDOM of thought and action. This is obtained, the subconscious states, through INVESTIGATION and EXPERIMENTATION.

Recreation, vacation—the subject should attempt to **work through play.**

Creative projects should NOT be neglected.

Now is the time to speculate, to take a chance, to seek SELF-EXPRESSION and personal advancement.

Personal magnetism, attractiveness are on the side of the subject at this time.

Write, communicate thoughts, dramatize, travel, open your heart—these are part of the over-all pattern, as indicated by the Thought Dial.

This is NOT the time to be confined, to stick to outmoded or so-called "proven" methods.

Number 5, as a total, LOOKS TO THE FUTURE through creativity.

Best advice: NOW IS THE TIME—do it!

IF THE TOTAL IS SIX:

Number 6 is similar, in some ways, to the digit 2. Number 6 is the diplomat, is associated with the planet Venus, has much to do with domesticity, conditions in the home, relations with relatives.

OFTEN, WHEN A SUBJECT DIALS A TOTAL OF 6, HE IS THINKING OF A CHANGE IN THE HOME. This change could be emotional, or an actual, physical move—a change of residence.

Whatever, it is necessary—with this total—for the subject to investigate family conditions, matters in his own home. It does no good to conquer the world, only to fail at home. Financial matters, marriage, contracts, public and home relations—all symbolized by this number.

The subject, through his subconscious, is being advised to be sympathetic. This is NOT the time to force issues, to be "tough." It is the time for handling persons and problems via diplomatic channels. Others depend on the subject for a sympathetic ear, a shoulder to cry on. SOMEONE CLOSE TO THE SUBJECT MAY FLAUNT THE LAWS OF CONVENTION. The subject, instead of being "shocked," or instead of preaching, should be DIPLOMATIC and SYMPATHETIC.

The elements are a **combination** of Earth and Air. And that tells a story: the subject, by dialing this total, knows that he must **combine** practicality with visionary foresight. That is the answer to all of his current problems: A COMBINATION OF EARTHINESS AND AIRY VISION.

Responsibility is a keynote. The weight of many problems—in connection with home, loved ones, family — rests on the subject's shoulders. HE SHOULD BE MADE TO SEE THAT THESE PROBLEMS WILL ALMOST SOLVE THEM-SELVES. He should not complicate them through forceful, or direct action. HE SHOULD LISTEN AND WAIT.

The subconscious mind, through the symbolism of the Thought Dial, tells the subject to take a stand for impartiality, for justice, for rational thinking. Otherwise, there are bound to be complications.

Number 6, quite often, is associated with the throat or voice. It is through **measured thought and speech** that the subject gains and is able to aid loved ones. Harmony is the desire here. To gain this harmony requires skill, diplomacy—and a sincere desire to see justice done.

THIS IS THE TIME (says the subconscious) TO SERIOUSLY CONSIDER MATTERS OF THE HOME . . . AS WELL AS MARRIAGE.

There is responsibility here. Just as with 5 there was romance . . . with 6 there is the responsibility of the home, of marriage, of the **results** of romance.

The subject is advised to be GENEROUS, both in willingness to negotiate disputes, to forgive errors, and to help those in financial need. There is a tendency here, as with the number 2, to collect, to be possesive. The subject must be on his guard, lest he fight for POSSESSIONS, for books he will never read, for dishes he will never use, and so on. COMMON SENSE—a sense of justice, maturity—these are the qualities that count now, that are very essential.

The subconscious, with this total, is urging restraint, pointing up the need to attend to matters at home, and is pushing forth for justice, compassion and diplomacy.

WAIT! BE PATIENT! AND REMEMBER THAT, RIGHT NOW, THE WORLD FOR YOU IS YOUR HOME!

IF THE TOTAL IS SEVEN:

Number 7 is associated with the planet Neptune: it is very similar in influence, in that the subject here is apt to be a victim of self-deception. It is not that others are trying to fool him, but he has a tendency to see persons and situations the way he wishes they could be, instead of the way they actually exist.

Number 7, as a total on the Thought Dial here, points to a basic loneliness. The subject is independent, sensitive, filled with pride. It is a matter of righting the world in his own mind, of convincing himself—when, all the time, it is ONLY IN HIS MIND.

No contracts here. No signing of legal documents. This is a time to wait and see. The subconscious, through the Thought Dial total, is trying to say that the aspects of the subject's life now are NEPTUNIAN. Which means there is a lack of solidity. This is a time for FAITH. But there is a fine line between faith, and willingness to FALL FOR A LINE. That's putting it roughly, perhaps, but it is the truth—and nothing could lead to disappointment and failure faster than contracts now, belief in those who offer only a so-called sincere front.

There is association, here, with hospitals, institutions: there is apt to be a feeling of confinement.

The tendency is to veer towards the romantic, to express willingness to go along with fantastic schemes. Thus, the obvious answer is to WAIT, especially in connection with partnerships, business-wise or in relation to marriage.

THIS IS THE TIME TO ANALYZE, TO PERFECT, TO EXAMINE, TO SCRUTINIZE PERSONS AND SITUATIONS. Take nothing for granted!

This is a time for critical SELF-EXAMINA-TION. This is the time for the subject to be ALONE. No one else can solve his problems. The solution comes from his INNER-SELF. Number 7, as a total, is not easy to comprehend because it represents a PERIOD OF TIME, or a thought, that is far from "easy." It is difficult, just as re-ligion, or inspiration, or intuition, is difficult to pin down or to evaluate on a material basis.

There is a desire for PERFECTION here, which can lead to brooding and worry. On the positive side, however, the subject can aim high—can do his best and achieve much—if he realizes that perfec-tion is not a necessity.

THE LESSON TO LEARN HERE IS TO BE ALONE WITHOUT SUFFERING THE PANGS OF LONELINESS.

The subject must be prepared to REJECT false flattery. He must be discriminating. For if he fails to SEEK the best, he will be unhappy.

As a subconscious total, number 7 (Water ele-ment) points up the necessity of eliminating persons and things NOT ESSENTIAL. The subject is be-ing told to TRIM DOWN. To get rid of waste. To accept solitude as something POSITIVE, not nega-tive. This is a SPIRITUAL number and symbol: it is a sure sign that the subject must re-evaluate his needs, desires, likes and dislikes. THE SUB-

JECT MUST GET TO KNOW HIMSELF. His outlook changes. His perspective improves.

IT IS ADVISABLE FOR HIM TO GET CLOSE TO NATURE AND ESPECIALLY TO HIS OWN NATURE.

No contacts here. Face reality. Avoid self-deception. Get off by yourself. Analyze—seek truth, perfection.

AND STOP BROODING!

IF THE TOTAL IS EIGHT:

This is the power number, associated with Saturn and pressure, responsibility—material gain is here, but along with it, plenty of hard work.

The element is Earth; the subject who dials this total as a subconscious indicator is concerned with finances, added responsibility, outside pressures perhaps involving marriage, members of the opposite sex and problems connected with business investments.

The subconscious, here, is saying, PUSH AHEAD, NOW IS THE TIME TO STRIKE! The Thought Dial (symbolizing the subconscious) urges action here, willingness to invest, to accept added pressures and responsibility—and that responsibility could be a new business, an investment, or marriage, or creative activity, including willingness to "have a child."

Number 8, perhaps, is one of the most powerful of the number symbols: it is sex, the creative urge, the giving of one's self.

THERE IS NOTHING HALFWAY HERE. IT IS ALL THE WAY OR NOTHING AT ALL. If the subject is wondering about putting a finger or a toe in—the Thought Dial tells him it is all the way, a complete dive in the water—or forget the project altogether.

Career, standing in the community, attainment of desires, a push up the ladder—all these things, and others, are symbolized by this total.

Lead without being the bully. Exercise authority without resorting to dictatorial methods. This is the executive number; the subject has asked for certain authority and has worked for it—now he has it and this is NO TIME TO SHIRK RESPON-SIBILITY.

Number 8 is 4 doubled, intensified. The details, it is assumed, have been taken care of, basic lessons learned. NOW IS THE TIME TO APPLY THOSE LESSONS, THAT KNOWLEDGE.

Avoid pettiness. Think and act big! That is the only way here, according to the message screamed by the subconscious.

The subject must be THE ORGANIZER. He must be prepared to grasp the most complicated situation at a glance. He should be urged to act upon his intuition, his judgment, his over-all knowledge. THIS IS NOT THE TIME TO BE SWAYED OR INFLUENCED BY SMALLER PERSONS.

Number 8 is money, finances, investments, building, commercial success, the marketing of material. The subject, here, must assume and **live** the role of EXECUTIVE.

The Earth and Saturn elements of the symbol, plus the Tenth House associations, show that the subject, to succeed, must push, must exercise power, must invest, advertise, work and organize.

Don't wait too long! And this applies to BOTH personal and business activities. MARRIAGE, BUSINESS. Those two sum up the keys to this symbol.

THIS IS THE TIME TO MAKE YOUR OWN

OPPORTUNITIES—that is the message of the Thought Dial.

The subject is not likely to succeed in a project that ALREADY HAS BEEN STARTED.

On the other hand, he DOES succeed in ORGANIZING a project himself, in taking a hank and a hair and some bones and putting together something that begins to PULSE WITH LIFE.

The symbol is clear enough. It is up to the subject to take note of the implications here. His subconscious tells him he is ready. NOW IS THE TIME FOR HIM TO BE CONVINCED THAT INDEED HE IS READY!

Remember, don't wait too long!

IF THE TOTAL IS NINE:

The subconscious, here, is making it plain that a situation, a relationship, a phase, a cycle of life, is COMPLETED. This is NOT the time to hang on. This IS the time to finish projects, to get rid of burdens which are not rightly the subject's responsibility in the first place.

Here, the subject—through his subconscious—is being told to seek new paths, new persons, new loves. The old is over. He must recognize this fact, no matter how difficult that task may be.

Number 9 is associated with the planet Mars, is of the Fire element, is related to personality, to independence in the spirit of breaking away from restrictions represented by the past.

If the subject is concerned about whether to begin a project, the answer is simple: DON'T!

If the subject is worried about whether to end a relationship, business or personal, the answer is equally simple: DO!

This, perhaps, is one of the clearest symbols.

THE SUBCONSCIOUS RELATES THE THEME OF PUBLIC RELATIONS on a UNIVERSAL SCALE. This IS the time to advertise, to let others know the value of products the subject has to offer.

Number 9 is the symbol of UNIVERSAL APPEAL. It is also, on the positive side, the number of selfless love. It is the number of the humanitarian, the nurse, doctor, teacher.

But, on the negative side, it tells a story of burden. Perhaps the subject is being taken advantage of by another: he is carrying someone else's financial load, pulling more, much more than his fair share. And this "pulling" can apply both to professional and personal matters. NOW IS THE TIME TO TAKE STOCK, TO MAKE A BREAK FOR NEW DIRECTIONS, FOR GREATER FREEDOM, PEACE OF MIND.

Simply put, the subconscious is strongly aware of a situation that no longer is tolerable. Perhaps the "situation" is represented by false hope, a false friend, a false promise. Or, perhaps the friend, the promise, the hope is sincere—but it will not work, not at this time. TO HANG ON WOULD BE TO IMPRISON ONE'S SELF.

This total on the Thought Dial, as a subconscious indicator, urges compassion—but a compassionate attitude based upon **practicality.** Now is the time for OTHERS TO HELP THEMSELVES. They can do this only if the subject REMOVES HIMSELF AS A CRUTCH.

Determination is required. It is certainly not easy to make a break, to take a new direction, a different course of action. Yet, it must be done! And it is to be done for the good of others, as well as for the subject's welfare.

In business matters, a relationship breaks up, but it is not a pretty sight because the break-up is not based on a mutual desire. Usually, it is the subject who must take the initiative.

THIS IS THE TIME—with this Thought Dial total—TO TRAVEL FAR AND WIDE . . . to seek new knowledge, to gain and adhere to a philosophy of life, one with enough fiber so that it does not tear at the slightest pull.

This is a summing up, the end of a cycle, preparation for the new.

FINISH. COMPLETE. SUMMARIZE. FINALIZE. These are keywords.

A long journey might well be in order here. Certainly, "journeys of the mind" are indicated, whether or not they take actual physical form.

DO NOT BROOD ABOUT THE PAST. LEARN FROM PAST EXPERIENCES AND APPLY THOSE LESSONS TO THE FUTURE.

And stop spoiling one you think you love!

IF THE TOTAL IS ELEVEN:

This is one of the two double numbers recognized in this system. Numbers 11 and 22 are not reduced to single digits. All others are. And so this number—11—is one of the most unusual of all: it represents a higher octave of 2, it is the Moon and Uranus, it is intuition and, most of all, it is the TEACHER. The subject, dialing this total on the Thought Dial, is concerned with UNSEEN FORCES. He is able to sense that something of importance is about to occur—but he can't quite put his finger on it.

As in number 2, diplomacy is called for. No forcing of issues. The element here is Air—motives must be of the highest order.

OTHERS WILL LOOK TO THE SUBJECT —then expect him to teach and, if necessary, to preach the law. Number 11 is similar to 7, in that religion in the highest sense of that word is involved. IF THE QUESTION IS WHETHER TO BY-PASS THE LAW, OR TO CLOSE ONE'S EYES TO SOMEONE WHO IS SKIRTING THE LAW—the answer is . . . DO NOT BECOME INVOLVED! Or, in plainer words, PLAY IT STRAIGHT!

If the subject is tempted to be weak here, he is warned (by the subconscious message) that he may get involved to a deeper extent than he dreamed possible. Hands off anything that isn't really honest to the letter. This applies to business and personal dealings—and to the subject's dealing with himself. CONSCIENCE is the keyword here. Pay attention to it!

The intuition is highlighted. THE SUBJECT, at this time, IS STRONGLY ADVISED TO TRUST HIS INTUITION. This is the time to hesitate, to listen to the INNER VOICE, to be cautious, to examine (and closely!) the motives of those who may be posing (or hiding) under the cloak of religion or charity, or otherwise. ASK THAT THE CARDS BE PLACED FACE UP ON THE TABLE!

This is the time, says the Thought Dial, to be IDEALISTIC.

This is the time to probe the unknown: interest indicated in astrology, electricity, television, aviation, outer space, the occult, extra-sensory perception, psychology, numerology, hand analysis, studies that lead to SELF-REVELATION.

YOU LEARN HERE BY TEACHING! Accept requests to be a GROUP LEADER. You advance by DOING.

The subject, dialing this total as a subconscious thought symbol, is concerned with a QUESTION OF FAITH. Faith in an individual, an idea, a government, a political party, a business enterprise—FAITH IN HIMSELF. In answer to this dilemma: LISTEN TO THE INNER VOICE, WHETHER YOU WISH TO CALL IT INTUITION OR CONSCIENCE, or whatever.

It is necessary for the subject to take time to KNOW HIMSELF. He must clear his mind of "clutterings" and get at his true source of inspiration.

The subject must go after SELF-RECOGNITION. He must first know himself before he can teach or help others. Otherwise, there will be unhappiness, self-annoyance, dissension.

In all, this is a powerful symbol: it is related to friends, hopes, wishes, children, relations with members of the opposite sex.

It is here, under this influence, that the subject asks himself concerning his lover: IS SHE MY FRIEND, TOO?

Much of the future depends upon the answer!

Don't rush into anything. When the tendency is to wait, to hesitate—do so.

IF THE TOTAL IS TWENTY-TWO:

This double number, like 11, is retained, instead of being reduced to a single digit, as other totals are—it is a master symbol in that it is the CREATIVE BUILDER. Number 22 appears to be related to the planet Pluto. The element here is Water. As a subconscious indicator on the Thought Dial, it tells of the necessity of thinking of projects as a WHOLE. The details, in this case, must be left to others: the subject cannot afford to be bogged down with matters of minor importance. The message here is simple: HAVE VISION, EXERCISE INTUITIVE INTELLECT — don't try to do everything yourself!

Number 22 is the master architect: it is a number of BUILDING. But the subject should realize that his subconscious is also telling him not to be afraid to TEAR DOWN.

Tear down and REBUILD, if necessary. This is no time to stick with a losing proposition—UNLESS YOU ARE PREPARED TO MAKE IMPROVEMENTS AND STREAMLINE THE OPERATION.

The subject, in dialing a total of 22, is expressing **subconscious knowledge** of this fact. He is capable of succeeding once this knowledge is MADE KNOWN TO HIS CONSCIOUS MIND, as it is being done here.

THIS IS THE TIME TO CARRY OUT IDEALS. This is the time, shouts the subconscious, to turn dreams into realities. Now is the time, without further delay, to put PLANS ON PAPER. Now—with all due speed—is the time to realize that inspiration is of solid substance and can be applied toward ultimate SUCCESS.

Number 22 is a symbol of success. That's why routine, details, must be left to others. The subject, dialing this total, must be the DREAMER OF PRACTICAL DREAMS. And that means he must MAKE his dreams COME TRUE.

This is **not** the time for false claims or false pride. This **is** the time to PRODUCE. Money will be forthcoming, perhaps from business or marital partners, from those who are inspired by the subject's FAITH and BELIEF.

In this way it can be seen that so-called INTANGIBLES help make the subject's dreams, visions, turn to REALITIES.

The subject is being told here that pettiness, inefficiency—both in his business and personal life—must be eliminated. The total of 22, as a subconscious symbol, warns that movements, campaigns, plans, ideas, hopes, wishes, must be on a GRAND SCALE. Anything small here seems doomed to failure. Even if the project is not a large one in a physical sense, it should be in an IDEALISTIC one.

Number 22 is a higher octave of 4. This presumes that the DETAILS are being well attended to, that associates can be trusted—that the subject has authority to BUILD UP, or TEAR DOWN, for the purpose of re-organizing. Otherwise, the subject should work to make these presumptions ACTU-ALITIES.

Diplomacy is necessary here. Intuition and sensitivity are also requisites. Ambition is keynoted. Where number 8 is concentrated, to a large extent, on FINANCIAL GAIN . . . 22 longs for RECOGNITION. There is much to live up to here. If the subject has been trying to SKIMP ON IDEALS . . . then he is not happy at this moment.

There is power here: the goal is the highest, but it can be reached. AND NO COMPROMISE SHOULD BE MADE!

That, perhaps, is the key to this symbol: The subject is being told that the time for compromise is **past**.

Move upward and onward. And if there is something, or someone blocking the way, build around, or over, or under—but build!

WHY AND HOW

In the previous section, detailed indications of what the subconscious tries to convey, through Thought Dial symbolism, were presented. Questions, of course, probably will continue to arise as to how and why the Thought Dial can be utilized as an instrument to impart this knowledge.

All of the answers are **not known.** But some of them are. As stated, the Thought Dial is based on the theory that memory **continues,** a sort of reflex action: memory always **being there,** even if the subject is **not** conscious of it.

Perhaps a good analogy would be a line—a time line. The beginning of the line is the past. The line continues to the **present,** and on to the **future.** The line has a beginning (the past), a middle, (the present) and an end (the future). Memory is like that line. It is there, from beginning to end, perhaps to infinity, as suggested by Dr. Joseph Rhine, of Duke University, whose experiments appear to verify Dr. Stromberg's belief that memory survives bodily death.

Memory is thus familiar with basic **number symbols,** the oldest symbols known to man, followed by symbols of an astrological nature.

In his syndicated newspaper feature, **Mirror of Your Mind,** (dated Feb. 4, 1958) Joseph Whitney asks: "Can memory be unconscious?" His answer is an unequivocal **yes.** He declares that unconscious memories influence many of our general behavior patterns. And he concludes by stating that, "Conscious memory influences behavior by direct recall, but unconscious memory does so without our awareness."

The unconscious memory, it can be presumed, is familiar with number symbols, seeking them out via the Thought Dial.

Now, it may be asked: "Who said numbers had any special meanings, anyhow?"

The answer to that can be found by consulting mathematicians who have made a serious study of numbers. Mr. Tobey, in his introduction, also goes into the story of numbers, their properties, meanings and personalities. Numerologists, too, although they are often frowned upon by academicians, have kept records for thousands of years, records based on research and experiments. The numbers, thus, have come to be associated with certain meanings, and the numbers stand as symbols, each telling a story with which **the subconscious is presumed to be familiar.**

Dr. Carl Jung has repeatedly asserted this to be true—that **planets and numbers** represent valuable keys to the unlocking of the subconscious.

It was the late Dr. Ernest Jones, biographer of Freud, who pointed out his subject's interest in the special meanings of numbers. He does so in his, **The Life and Work of Sigmund Freud.*** In that distinguished work, Dr. Jones reveals Freud's fascination with parapsychology, including psychoanalysis and telepathy, and dreams and telepathy. Freud's greatest student, of course, was Jung, who constantly pleaded the case of astrology—and continues with a lively interest in the subject. Freud himself ascribed special powers to numbers and declared that the figures 28 and 23 were important in his own life.

These are some of the answers—or at least **hints**

*Basic Books, Inc., New York

of what the answers **might** be—in the "why and how" of the Thought Dial.

Just as it is possible to cultivate the "mind's eye" (create mental images, develop a strong mental, visual sense), so it is also possible to cultivate the subconscious and its familiarity with well-known symbols (numbers and planets).

In his article, **You Can Cultivate the Mind's Eye,*** Bruce Bliven points out that capable mathematicians usually have a strong visual sense. Bliven, in his study, says mathematicians are able to picture complicated problems. He presents, as an example, mathematician John von Neumann, who apparently could "see" the final result of a long problem—see it written in his mind.

Perhaps the subconscious **is** the "mind's eye." It enables us to "see" when we give it the opportunity of expressing itself through numbers (Thought Dial).

*The Diplomat, Diplomat Publishing Co., Washington, D.C. (Dec., 1957)

DIRECT QUESTIONS ANSWERED

In the section on subconscious thoughts, general indications were given for the various Thought Dial totals. In many instances, these **general** analyses **will** provide not only the answer to specific problems, but also cover numerous other current aspects of the subject's life.

However, to be more specific, the Thought Dial can be applied to the answering of **special** problems. At times, the answers will dovetail or coincide with the subconscious indicator. That is, a total of 9—dialed with a **specific** problem in mind, will be similar to the 9 total as a subconscious indicator. This is as it should be.

It is interesting to note that, many times, when the subject thinks of a direct or specific question, he also reveals **the birthdate** of a person concerned in the question. Other times, through the Thought Dial, he gives his **own** zodiacal sign.

For example, the subject thinks of a specific question. At all times, the question should be formed clearly, as briefly as possible. Then, after the subject concentrates, he is to dial three numbers. The operator then totals and reduces to a single number, unless the total happens to be 11 or 22.

Suppose the total, in this instance, is 2. Number 2 is associated with the Moon, which rules Cancer. The subject himself, or one important to his question or problem, can be presumed (many times) to be born under Cancer, between June 22nd and July 23rd, OR UNDER THE OPPOSITE SIGN: CAPRICORN (from December 22nd to January 20th).

In other words, the total on the Thought Dial reveals a significant birthdate in relation to the subject's problem or question. The birthdates revealed are as follows:

IF THE TOTAL IS 1: Leo or Aquarius—From July 24th to August 23rd or from January 21st to February 19th.

IF THE TOTAL IS 2: Cancer or Capricorn—From June 22nd to July 23rd, or from December 22nd to January 20th.

IF THE TOTAL IS 3: Sagittarius or Gemini—From November 23rd to December 21st, or from May 22nd to June 21st.

IF THE TOTAL IS 4: Aquarius or Leo—From January 21st to February 19th, or from July 24th to August 23rd.

IF THE TOTAL IS 5: Gemini or Sagittarius—From May 22nd to June 21st, or from November 23rd to December 21st; or Virgo or Pisces (August 24 to September 23rd — February 20th to March 20th).

IF THE TOTAL IS 6: Taurus or Scorpio—From April 21st to May 21st, or from October 24th to November 22nd; or Libra or Aries (September 24th to October 23rd — March 21st to April 20th).

IF THE TOTAL IS 7: Pisces or Virgo—From February 20th to March 20th, or from August 24th to September 23rd.

IF THE TOTAL IS 8: Capricorn or Cancer—From December 22nd to January 20th, or from June 22nd to July 23rd.

IF THE TOTAL IS 9: Aries or Libra—From March 21st to April 20th, or from September 24th to October 23rd.

IF THE TOTAL IS 11: Aquarius or Leo—from

January 21st to February 19th, or from July 24th to August 23rd, or Cancer or Capricorn—from June 22nd to July 23rd, or December 22nd to January 20th.

IF THE TOTAL IS 22: Scorpio or Taurus— From October 24th to November 22nd, or from April 21st to May 21st.

Now, not in all cases will the birthdate revealed appear significant. In many cases, however, it is either the subject's own zodiacal sign, or belongs to a person currently significant in the question, or one **who will be in the future.**

With practice in delineation, the operator of the Thought Dial will develop skill, just as in the case of interpreting a horoscope.

These interpretations, which follow, provide a cornerstone, a starting point, a basis — a basis evolved after some ten years of experiment and research.

I have found that these basic interpretations work. Clients or subjects are aided. The operator, using this system, often finds a key and looks for certain things in the horoscope, or personality makeup of the subject. The Thought Dial leads the way. From there on, it is necessary for the operator to develop skill. And it is up to the subject to analyze and derive what benefits he can from Thought Dial indications.

Remember, the subject must concentrate on a SPECIFIC question. He must form it clearly, concisely in his own mind. When he has done this, he is to dial three numbers on the Thought Dial. The operator then totals the digits, reducing the answer to a single number between 1 and 9, with the exceptions of 11 or 22, which are the only double numbers not reduced. The subject THINKS and DIALS; he does **not** reveal his question.

IF THE TOTAL IS 1:

Specifically, the subject's question concerns a new project, or a new association, either business or personal. In many cases, the subject has met someone and is romantically inclined toward that person. The subconscious, through the Thought Dial, encourages the subject to pursue NEW PERSONS, PROJECTS, and paths that lead to greater independence of thought and action through a BREAK WITH THE PAST.

Significant zodiacal signs, in connection with this question, are apt to be LEO or AQUARIUS.

The question itself is one which evolves around initiative, creative ability, new starts, original thinking, and could be associated with affairs of the heart. Children, too, might well be involved.

The closest to a direct answer would be: GO YOUR OWN WAY ON THIS MATTER. It is not a time to follow others. Rather, the Thought Dial indicates that only through direct, original, perhaps daring action, can you succeed.

The question, most likely, is one which involves pioneering action. And the subject is apt to be concerned with a BREAK FROM TRADITION.

The answer, provided by the subconscious (via the Thought Dial), is that a break is necessary for a positive conclusion to this problem.

The subject wants to know whether to go back, or to move ahead. The answer is to MOVE AHEAD.

Children, entertainment, creative ways of entertaining are also suggested. New ways to advertise. New ways to serve in the entertainment fields—all these are favored in answer to the question being asked.

The subject should, in dialing this total, be encouraged to emerge as an INDIVIDUAL who LEADS the way.

A direct answer would be, YES—go ahead! Be confident that original, forceful methods will work in this case. No turning back, not now!

IF THE TOTAL IS 2:

The subject himself was born under Cancer or Capricorn, or someone important in this question might have been born under one of those zodiacal signs. The question itself is one which covers the areas of SECURITY, HOME, ONE OF THE PARENTS. In dialing this total, the subject shows he is much aware of a need for security, a bank account, the collecting of data which will enable him to prove his worth.

One part of the answer to this question is: STOP BROODING! Worry here can only hinder, not help. And the subject, as his subconscious reveals, has been doing a lot of worrying, much of it needless.

In answer to the question: The subject must collect data, facts, and he must also be prepared to accept a budget. There will be limitations to what he can do. BUT HE CAN BEST SUCCEED BY GOING ALONG WITH THE TIDE, by **quiet acceptance.** There is no better time to be a diplomat than in connection with this problem!

Someone in his own home can help the subject. And, in answer to the question, the **answer is not to try to answer at this time.** Wait. Be patient. Let the storm blow over. Hold the line. Prepare a presentation of the facts and, when called upon, present them with diplomacy and modesty.

In other words, the time for decision has NOT YET ARRIVED. This is the time for watchful waiting—but NOT for brooding.

A woman, an older woman, appears to figure prominently in the outcome of this problem.

The subconscious stresses the need for careful consideration of the future. This can be done, first, by working out a budget and sticking to it.

IF THE TOTAL IS 3:

CONFUSION is the keyword here. In answer to the subject's question, nothing can be accomplished until he settles down. It does no good to try probing in all directions at once. Wasted energy indicated here, in a question related to long journeys, ideas of an expansive nature, and to social activities. Public relations, advertising—and persons (perhaps the subject himself) born under the zodiacal signs of Sagittarius or Gemini—may all be involved in the answer to this query.

The outcome appears favorable, whatever the question, because the subconscious cries only for STEADINESS, a veering AWAY from confusion —and does NOT cry in anything resembling panic.

The subject, dialing this total, does not appear to know JUST WHAT IT IS he wants. Curiosity runs high. And the question, very likely, has to do with the possibility of FINDING OUT MORE— possibly the **theme** of the query has to do with social activities, and most certainly it concerns one who is far away, or is planning to move away.

A sense of humor is a necessity if the subject is to arrive at a constructive solution. Otherwise, he is apt to create trouble where none existed.

OFTEN A SUBJECT WHO IS MERELY TESTING THE DIAL—one who has a pre-determined attitude that there is "nothing to it"—will dial a 3 total. This is the subconscious symbol of little or no concentration. The answer to the question—if one actually is being asked—also lies in this sphere: a call for greater concentration, attention to details, and an attitude based on facts, not fancy.

The problem or question here is NOT as serious as the subject might believe. And circumstances may well take it out of his hands before he can do anything about it.

IF THE TOTAL IS 4:

The answer to this question is more work; the subject cannot "escape" from the routine which he is coming to abhor. Now is not the time.

Either the subject himself, or one closely related to the problem, was born under Aquarius, or perhaps under the zodiacal sign of Leo. Hoping and wishing will not make it so. Passing the buck won't, either. There are details, many of them considered unpleasant, which have to be attended to before anything else can be accomplished.

Specifically, the question concerns a "blocking in," restriction, a lack of freedom—the lack caused either by a person or situation, or both.

The answer, based on the 4 symbol, lies with the subject: he must make up his mind to finish what was started.

No, don't trust details to others.

Yes, do prepare to work hard and harder—there is a square, a block which stands in the way, an obstacle: this is a test and to be a test of any value it must test you. Knowing this, the subject should be prepared to WORK and WAIT.

No, do not make sudden changes

Yes, do plan for a change in the FUTURE.

You are not imprisoned. You make your own prison by feeling that all avenues to escape are sealed.

The answer, in general, is negative—BUT ONLY FOR THE TIME BEING!

The subject is concerned with LACK: lack of finances, lack of love, lack of freedom, lack of appreciation, and the list could be extended. BUT THE ANSWER LIES IN PATIENCE, GRIT. DETERMINATION, WILLINGNESS TO DO THE RIGHT THING AND SEE THE PROJECT THROUGH TO ITS COMPLETION.

The solution here could come through a younger person, perhaps one of the subject's own children. A loved one aids here—and the subject is grateful he waited.

The answer is WAIT.

And no excuses!

IF THE TOTAL IS 5:

The subject, thinking of a specific question and dialing this total, is apt to have sex on his mind!

That is, the subject is concerned with a member of the opposite sex: the subconscious, via this symbol, reveals that creativity, including love, creative thinking, etc., is necessary to the solution of the problem.

The answer is generally affirmative. Marriage is strongly indicated. So is change, travel, communication of thoughts through writing or the other arts.

Yes, now is the time to expand and experiment.

No, now is **not** the time to practice enforced economy. The BUDGET must be STRETCHED!

The zodiacal signs involved here are Gemini and Sagittarius, and Virgo and Pisces.

Love and marriage highlighted. But the subject, if he is specifically asking about marriage, should make sure there is MORE THAN JUST PHYSICAL ATTRACTION INVOLVED. Otherwise, he will find that the honeymoon is soon over.

The subconscious, through this symbol, seems to be telling of the necessity to COMMUNICATE, to travel, even though the journeys be short ones, to "keep in touch" with friends, relatives, those who have—in the recent past—been neglected by the subject.

Yes, express yourself by writing, by INVESTING IN YOUR OWN TALENTS.

NO, do not listen to those who are urging you to wait, to pull a surprise in the future. NOW IS THE TIME, not later.

The answer to the question, put simply, is: MAKE A CHANGE, even if travel is involved. AND DON'T RUN AWAY FROM ROMANCE. You will only have to return!

In conclusion, calm down! The number 5 symbol is indicative that the subject is "keyed up."

Self-expression is the best way of getting rid of this tension.

IF THE TOTAL IS 6:

Persons dialing this total, very often, are concerned with a domestic situation. THE DIRECT ANSWER TO THE QUESTION IS: A change in the home, through adjustment or readjustment, is very necessary. Putting off the situation will not help. It will, instead, aggravate the problem.

Too, there is apt to be concern with the voice in some manner or other.

Basically, it is a matter of rediscovering loved ones. Of adjusting to their needs. Of clearing up a situation in the home that has been allowed to hang on and on.

Yes, DO move, if that seems to be the only solution. Yes, a change of residence is apt to prove beneficial.

Straighten out family differences. The answer to the question is generally NEGATIVE—but only until those matters involving family and home are attended to—then the situation brightens.

Birthdates (zodiacal signs) involved in this question appear to be: Taurus and Scorpio—Libra and Aries.

Money matters could be involved here because a move, a "brightening" of the atmosphere through decorations, fixtures, new furniture, appear necessary.

DRAMA AND VOICE—artistic expression— these, too, come through as a result of this subconscious symbol. Perhaps a member of the subject's family—or the subject himself—is concerned with these matters.

There are some loose ends which need tying: the subject, if he seeks a solution by further delay, is in for a rude shock. NOW IS THE TIME TO STRAIGHTEN O U T MATTERS I N T H E HOME. Now, not later.

A plea that "these things cost money" is a poor excuse.

The answer to this question lies in direct action to remedy an oversight which, long ago, should have been remedied.

IF THE TOTAL IS 7:

This, it appears, is a case of self-deception. It isn't that others are attempting to fool the subject or to mislead him: but, in connection with this question, he seems intent on fooling **himself.**

Zodiacal signs involved here are Pisces and Virgo.

A relationship appears to be breaking up: a contract is not valid. The answer to the question, briefly stated—is YES **and** NO.

No, your ideas about a person or situation will not hold water. In the near future your illusions will be shattered.

Yes, you will recover, and go on to fulfill your mission, your hopes and your wishes.

You will do this by ridding yourself of false concepts. You will be in a better position to face reality once a Neptunian situation is eliminated.

You will gain **inner strength** through present trials. There is a feeling of restriction here. The subject is apt to find himself confined due to a minor illness: his freedom of movement is hampered, sometimes because of a foot injury.

In answer to the question: GET TO KNOW YOURSELF FIRST. BE SURE YOU KNOW WHAT IT IS YOU ACTUALLY DESIRE. The indications are that present relationships—the ones you are asking about—are based to a great degree on wishful thinking.

Illusion is the keyword. The answer to this question is favorable if the subject happens to be in the film business, as producer, actor, writer, etc. Or if he is associated with television—the visual arts. Otherwise, the indications are that this question is based upon dream-like qualities which, however beautiful, have nothing to do with practical living.

Avoid signing contracts. Remember, if you are asking about an individual, he may be well-intentioned—but he does NOT appear to be for you.

The number 7 symbol, as an indicator of your question, reveals that you are concerned with a person, or situation; the relationship does not seem destined to last.

Learn everything you can while it does continue. Then, get off by yourself. You have a lot to learn about you!

IF THE TOTAL IS 8:

The question here concerns money matters, responsibility, perhaps marriage; emphasis certainly seems to lie on finance and concern over finances due to added pressure, responsibility and an additional mouth to feed.

Birth signs involved are Capricorn and Cancer.

The subject, dialing 8 as an indicator for a direct question, is asking about business matters and is concerned about authority, responsibility and the money to run things as he would like to, or has been ordered to: number 8 is this kind of symbol and has much to do with standing in the community and with AMBITION.

The answer, generally, is YES. Accept added responsibility because there is no constructive way to avoid it. The answer, too, is NO, in that this project will be no bed of roses. THERE IS WORK TO BE DONE AND NOW IS THE TIME TO ACCEPT AND MEET A CHALLENGE.

Commercial enterprises are favored only if the subject realizes the necessity of WORK and INVESTMENT. Nothing half-way will do here. There is no putting one foot in the water to see if it is too cold. It is all the way or nothing at all.

In matters of a personal nature—there is no experimenting, no hitting and running. ONCE THE SUBJECT BECOMES INVOLVED HERE, IT IS ALL THE WAY, probably marriage or children, or both.

In matters of a business nature—the same implies. Losses are incurred unless the subject is prepared to devote FULL TIME to the project.

YES, do invest. YES, do marry and get engaged or continue the romance. YES, do these things— if you are mature enough to face a big challenge

and to face a battle without running for cover.

The question or problem being thought of here is of a serious nature. If the subject is not **consciously** aware of this fact, his **subconscious** most decidedly is, and is trying (through the Thought Dial) to tell him so.

Build, invest, advertise, let loved ones know you care.

Sex, in a creative, mature sense, plays an important role here.

The answer to the question is WORK.

The subject will meet with emotional and professional failure unless he is willing to WORK.

IF THE TOTAL IS 9:

A relationship, a cycle, much of the recent past —is coming to an end—and the answer to the question is BREAK AWAY FROM THE OLD AND TAKE THE ROAD TOWARD A NEW DIRECTION AND LIFE.

Yes, be willing to break off.

Yes, you are right in sensing you have been carrying another's rightful responsibility.

Yes, be a humanitarian and a nurse and a teacher and lend a helping hand—but DRAW THE LINE AT BEING "USED," AT BEING TAKEN ADVANTAGE OF BY PERSONS WHO ARE IN THE HABIT OF HAVING YOU DO THE UNPLEASANT TASKS.

Birth signs involved are Aries and Libra.

In answer to this question: Past associations, partnerships—business and personal—have outlived their usefulness. A NEW APPROACH is required here. Proper perspective is being called for by the subconscious via this symbol.

Direct, independent, forceful action is required on the part of the subject. Otherwise, he will be unhappy, he will lag behind, he will lose much in both a professional and a personal sense.

A RELATIONSHIP IS TERMINATING. It is NOT beginning, no matter how things appear on the surface (to the conscious mind). The subconscious clearly states that an influence is fading out of the subject's life. Fresh, original ideas are needed here.

This is the time, in relation to this particular question, to ADVERTISE, to let many (instead of few) know of your capabilities. GOOD PUBLIC RELATIONS IS ESSENTIAL FOR A SUCCESSFUL OUTCOME OF THIS PROBLEM.

Generally, the answer is in the affirmative. Specifically, BREAK FROM THE OLD—take the initiative and LEAD THE WAY. Try something NEW!

To successfully resolve this question, insist on originality and let others carry their own load.

IF THE TOTAL IS 11:

Birth signs involved are AQUARIUS and LEO, CANCER and CAPRICORN.

IN ANSWER TO THE QUESTION: Trust your intuition!

Intuitive intellect is required here. No outsider can provide the right advice, no matter how logical that counsel may appear. The subconscious, by delivering this symbol, is asking to take over. The problem here is one involving EMOTIONS. As such, application and consideration of PURELY FACTUAL material is not apt to be of much aid.

Best advice, in relation to your question: BE IDEALISTIC. Stick to your ideals. Do not lower your sights. Refuse to be influenced by those who, however well meaning, try to get you to be "practical." What they actually mean, is "practical" through their eyes, the way they see the question. WHAT YOUR SUBCONSCIOUS TELLS YOU IS FOR YOUR BENEFIT AND THAT IS OF IMPORTANCE HERE.

An affair of the heart seems to be involved in this question. What is to be avoided is an attitude that leads to brooding, to depression and defeatism. IF NECESSARY, MAKE A SUDDEN MOVE: put your cards on the table and call the bluff!

Eventually, as this problem is resolved, YOU WILL BE THE TEACHER. Your advice will be followed. There is reluctance—on the surface. BUT YOU CAN WIN OUT. Keep this thought in mind. It is one your subconscious is attempting to filter through to your conscious mind. Be AWARE of your potential.

A child may be involved, or those who are dependent upon the subject. These considerations are important—and the subject should follow his heart in this matter. ANY OTHER WAY LEADS TO UNHAPPINESS.

The answer is generally negative, but ONLY IN A TEMPORARY SENSE. By hanging on—and remaining true to INTUITION and IDEALS—the subject eventually wins.

IF THE TOTAL IS 22:

Birth signs involved in this question are SCORPIO and TAURUS.

In answer to the question: CREATIVITY AND A SENSE OF "BUILDING" ARE ALL-IMPORTANT.

Although the answer is generally negative, the FINAL outcome is of a POSITIVE nature.

This appears contradictory on the surface. But,

in reality, it is simply a matter of OVERCOMING ROUTINE OBSTACLES—and getting down to work on CREATIVE projects.

The subconscious, in offering this "master symbol," clearly indicates that the subject need worry **only as long as he remains bogged down with feelings of insecurity.**

Yes, now is the time to BUILD.

NO, now is not the time to go back over details, to be disturbed by associates who are dominated by the petty, the inconsequential.

YES, tear down in order to REBUILD.

NO, do not let others talk you into a "smaller investment."

YES, do see the project (possibilities for the future) as a whole.

HAVE VISION!

Vision will provide needed confidence. Sure, the task, the ideal is huge in score: BUT THE SUBJECT IS CAPABLE OF COMING UP WITH THE RIGHT ANSWERS (talent and creative ability and hard work).

Money may be forthcoming from a marriage or business partner.

Inspiration demands upon the subject's FREEDOM. Thus, he should not allow himself to be tied down by promises of economy.

Refuse to budge if an idea must crumple as a result.

THE FUTURE HOLDS A SMILE FOR THE SUBJECT. He should give it a chance to show!

YES AND NO TECHNIQUE

This section is inspired by Dr. Marc Edmund Jones' superb reference work on horary astrology*—in which Dr. Jones discusses the "yes and no technique" in interpreting horary charts. That technique, I consider, invaluable. It gets to the essence of horary astrology, the very purpose for its existence: to provide direct, concise answers to specific questions.

This technique, utilized in connection with the Thought Dial, should be looked upon in the proper perspective: it is like the light provided from a struck match as compared to a shining electric bulb. The flare of the match enables the subject to get his bearings, so to speak. The "struck match" is the yes and no technique as applied to the Thought Dial. However, for "prolonged light," the sections on **Subconscious Thoughts** and **Direct Questions Answered** are necessary.

Thus, for so-called "minor questions," or quick insights, the yes and no technique is valid.

The subject thinks of a question with a "yes" or "no" answer, then dials three numbers, reducing the total to a single number (unless the total happens to add to 11 or 22).

IF THE TOTAL IS 1:
    YES—definite.

IF THE TOTAL IS 2:
    NO—definite.

*Available from Llewellyn Publications, Ltd., Los Angeles 34.

IF THE TOTAL IS 3:
  YES—less definite.

IF THE TOTAL IS 4:
  NO—less definite.

IF THE TOTAL IS 5:
  YES—definite.

IF THE TOTAL IS 6:
  NO—definite.

IF THE TOTAL IS 7:
  NO—but a "yes" is indicated after some delay.

IF THE TOTAL IS 8:
  NO—but a "yes" is indicated soon.

IF THE TOTAL IS 9:
  YES—but along different lines. New ideas needed.

IF THE TOTAL IS 11:
  NO—but something better is forthcoming.

IF THE TOTAL IS 22:
  YES—definite.

LOCATING LOST ARTICLES

This section, as well as the next—PICKING WINNERS—must rightfully be categorized as in the field of the speculative. That is, speculative in relation to the previous parts of this work. Through what research that has ensued, it is felt that those portions dealing with **subconscious thoughts, questions answered,** and the **yes and no technique,** are more than speculations. The material contained in those sections is presented as work that has been tested and which has yielded promising results—results, in most cases, as satisfactory as any astrological or general psychological technique. Admittedly, more work, additional research is required before we know what it is we have here in the Thought Dial. The same is true of any technique dealing with human beings, their actions and reactions, particularly their thoughts—and, more specifically, their **inner** thoughts. That is why this volume is being released at this time. I have, as an individual, gone as far as I can—alone. It is with a great deal of certainty that I state that further experiments, performed by those in possession of this work, will enlighten us to a greater degree —perhaps beyond our most optimistic expectations.

That is why it is necessary to differentiate between what has gone forth and what is now being presented. The **theory** is basically the same. Nothing is "lost." The subconscious, or some part of our selves, **knows** where the item, or object, has been placed (or misplaced). **Or whether the object is not to be found by the subject.** This technique has been utilized in horary astrology. It has been used, too, in connection with numbers. I am indebted to Sepharial and his work, **The Kabala of Numbers***

*David McKay Company, New York (1945)

for much of the information provided here.

INSTRUCTIONS: Subject thinks of the object he wishes to locate: when a clear picture of the object is obtained, or when the question of "Where is it?" is formed, three numbers are dialed on the Thought Dial. As in previous instances, the numbers (with the exceptions of 11 and 22) are reduced to a single digit between 1 and 9.

IF THE TOTAL IS 1:

The object is, most likely, in a main part of a house: the living room or bedroom. Sepharial suggests that it may well be found in a room near white linen. He recommends, too, that a fair child be questioned.

Direction: SOUTH.

It would appear* that the object was lost while the subject (or whoever **did** lose it) was in pursuit of pleasure: a hunting trip, a picnic, etc. It would appear that the object **will** be found.

IF THE TOTAL IS 2:

Specifically, Sepharial declares the object is to be found in a house, in a vase or bowl, or close by. Indications are that someone will aid in finding the thing lost, perhaps a maid or housekeeper, or a cook.

Direction: SOUTH.

The object lost **will** be found.

IF THE TOTAL IS 3:

The object being sought may be located in a passage or between papers. It could well be found in a place where men congregate.

*Besides material provided by Sepharial, reference is made here, as with other symbols, to rules set forth by William Lilly, in 1647, in his classic work, **Lilly's Introduction to Astrology.**

Direction: NORTH.

Indications are that carelessness was involved in this loss, not necessarily carelessness on the part of the subject—but on the part of one he trusts.

The general indication is that the article will be found.

IF THE TOTAL IS 4:

For this total, Sepharial states, "The article is in your possession, and is not lost."

Assuming, however, that the article is not in the subject's possession, the direction is likely to be toward the NORTHEAST. Indications are that the article will be recovered.

It would appear, from this total on the Thought Dial, that the object has been misplaced due to absent-mindedness on the part of the subject. A number of other details appear to occupy his attention—then, bolt-like—he remembers a series of events which lead to recovery of the lost object.

IF THE TOTAL IS 5:

Sepharial suggests: "Look under a hat, turban, or other headgear." The indications are that the object will be found—once the subject stops looking.

Direction: Toward the WEST.

It appears that the object was lost while the subject was in transit: travel, communications—perhaps the mailing of a letter—all might be involved here.

IF THE TOTAL IS 6:

The object, according to Sepharial, might be found where sandals or boots are kept. The possibility is strong that the thing being sought is on a shelf, or a stand of some kind.

The direction is either to the extreme EAST or WEST.

The odds of finding this lost object are **not** great.

IF THE TOTAL IS 7:

Sepharial specifically states, "Ask your servant, a maid especially connected with the wardrobe."

The direction is EAST.

The indications are that the object will **not** be found. It is most likely in a place associated with water. There is deception indicated here, indicative of the fact that someone is withholding information, thus lessening the odds of recovering what is lost.

IF THE TOTAL IS 8:

Someone else may find this, but it is **not** likely the subject will be directly responsible. Sepharial states the lost object may be on a shelf or horizontal ledge.

The direction is NORTH.

Illness of some sort (specifically a cold or ailment affecting the bones) appears to be connected with this loss.

The object may be in a field—possibly where cattle graze.

IF THE TOTAL IS 9:

According to Sepharial: "A child has it among some clothing." The indications are that the object **will** be recovered.

The direction is EAST.

This object may have been lost due to a quarrel. That is, the subject—in a state of anger or excitement—unknowingly discarded it, perhaps in a fire, where it was subsequently recovered by a young person.

IF THE TOTAL IS 11:

Quoting Sepharial: "You must take a short journey to a tank, pool, or stretch of water."

The direction is NORTHEAST.

It would appear that this object was lost at a resort, or where people go to relax: a swimming pool, a night club, perhaps a private party where "liquid" was being dispensed.

Much effort will have to be exerted if this object is to be recovered.

The manner in which it was lost might prove embarrassing; the subject may wish to forget the matter.

IF THE TOTAL IS 22:

Sepharial states flatly: "The thing is on a shelf in the house, and will be speedily found."

The direction is WEST.

Indications are that it **will** be found.

The kitchen or bathroom would appear to be the site.

The subject should avoid hasty conclusions or accusations.

PICKING WINNERS

Perhaps I should begin this section by quoting from the column of Matt Weinstock, dated March 7, 1958, which appeared in the **Mirror News,** of Los Angeles. It reads:

> "So you don't believe the stars can influence people's lives? Some people do, among them writer Sydney Omarr, who insists astrology is an authentic science.

> "Syd was interviewed on Ben Hunter's early morning KFI program and when Ben said he was going to Santa Anita that day Syd suggested a test based on a chapter titled, 'How to Pick Winners' in his book 'Thought Dial'.

> "Syd asked him to concentrate on going to the cashier's window after a race and collecting money, then to pick horses based on a numerical sequence whose names reminded him of the Sun.

> "Ben bet a horse across the board in each of six races and all six finished in the money."

Yes, that's what happened. Ben Hunter, who conducts a "Night Owl" radio program in Los Angeles, tested the Thought Dial on the air. He selected three numbers which, when added and reduced to a single digit, equalled 1. Number 1, of course, is associated with the Sun. First, as Matt Weinstock reports, Ben had concentrated on **winning.** He had the thought clearly formed in his mind when he selected three numbers. Since the numbers added to 1 (all double numbers, with the exception of 11 and 22, are reduced to a single digit between 1 and 9), he was told to select horses whose names reminded **him,** or suggested to **him,** the **symbols** of number 1: the Sun, pioneer, new starts, originality, creativity, etc. Number 1, being associated with the Sun, is also related to the zodiacal sign of Leo (especially good for speculation, being the natural fifth sign in the zodiac), and so names related to that sign would also have been significant.

It would be too much to hope for the kind of success Ben Hunter obtained in picking winners with the Thought Dial. However, there is reason to believe that, through use of the Thought Dial (free utilization of "subconscious knowledge"). the average of winners will be greater. Anecdotes about persons who are able to "win on paper," but not when they are actually betting money at the track, are numerous. Too numerous to be mere coincidences. There is a pattern there, in those stories of persons who are able to mastermind a football game, or a race track competition, or other event, but who, when it comes to picking winners with cash on the line, "freeze up" or allow themselves to be "touted off" their original selections. Why does this happen?

It happens, in all probability, because the conscious or "censor" mind stands in the way when pressure is applied: there is too much rationalizing, too much thinking, or what passes for thinking and what, in all likelihood, is a "pinching off" of the flow from the subconscious. In other words, sitting at home with his newspaper list of competitors, a man is able to relax (knowing he is not going to risk money, anyway) and choose. The same man, whose average is high "on paper," seems to lose his canny sense once his own money is on the line at the track. This is because he is too conscious of what he is doing; he is trying to be logical and, perhaps, logic is a detriment in this sort of thing. Detriment or not—or whatever—it would appear (as in the striking example of Ben Hunter's success) that once the subject is relaxed enough, or "unaware enough," his subconscious makes itself felt and he fares better.

This boils down to the theory that the subconscious is able to **perceive** the future or is **aware** of it: it is the case of the "time line" once more, with the supposition that the subconscious is able to see the beginning, middle and end of it. If we will only let it!

Dr. Rhine, I am sure, would attribute this "ability to see" to extra-sensory perception. Specifically he would term this section an experiment in **precognition**. That is, the ability to "recognize" a future event before it occurs. Dr. Rhine may be right: the subconscious may, after all, have nothing whatever to do with foretelling the future. But, then again, there may be more of an association between the subconscious and ESP than any of us know. The point being made here . . . is that no matter **why** or **how** the Thought Dial works, the important thing is that it **does**. So, in the long run, it does not matter (for our purposes) whether the symbols are presented to us by the subconscious or by ESP. What **does** matter is that, through the Thought Dial, **some** element within ourselves is tapped, and we are thus able to "see" to a greater extent.

In picking winners, the subject concentrates **on the outcome** of the contest. If it is a horse race, he should think of collecting money at the end of the race: he must picture himself at the pari-mutuel window, holding a winning ticket. With this thought clearly in mind, he dials three numbers and, in the usual manner, reduces the total to a single number between 1 and 9 (with the exceptions of 11 and 22, the only double numbers retained as totals).

The symbols represented by the total dialed provide the winners. It needn't be a horse race. The process of "picking winners" with the Thought Dial

can be applied to boxing matches, football or baseball games, perhaps even political contests! If the
Thought Dial comes up with an individual's zodiacal sign—then pick that person, by all means!
That is, if in a boxing match, one fighter was born
under Capricorn, another under Cancer, and the
Thought Dial total was 8, then the Capricorn boxer
would be selected (number 8 associated with Saturn; and that planet rules Capricorn).

An explanation of how the Thought Dial, on
occasion, reveals birth dates of individuals is provided in the section, "Direct Questions Answered."

All right—we're ready now for the symbols
associated with various Thought Dial totals. The
list provided here is by no means complete. It is
hoped that readers, upon experimenting, will develop key words of their own.

Reminder: Think of yourself as having picked
the winner: the contest or competition is over, and
you have chosen the right animal, athlete, political
candidate, etc. With this thought clearly in mind,
start dialing.

IF THE TOTAL IS 1:

Number 1 is associated with the Sun and the
zodiacal sign of Leo the Lion.

Key words: SUN, INDEPENDENCE, LEAD-
ER, ORIGINALITY, SPECULATION, LOVE,
THEATER, BELLE OF THE BALL, EGO,
CHILDREN, AND ANYTHING NEW, START-
LING OR SEXY.

This number, in picking winners, is considered
fortunate.

IF THE TOTAL IS 2:

Number 2 is associated with the Moon and the
zodiacal sign of Cancer the Crab.

Key words: MOON, BROODING, HOME, SECURITY, THE WOMAN IN YOUR LIFE, MOTHER, INSANITY, THE PUBLIC, PATRIOTISM, COMFORT, DIPLOMACY, AND ANYTHING ASSOCIATED WITH A SENSE OF SAFETY AS PROVIDED BY PARENTS OR HOME.

This number, in picking winners, is **not** as fortunate as some others.

IF THE TOTAL IS 3:

Number 3 is associated with the planet Jupiter and the zodiacal sign of Sagittarius the Archer.

Key words: LUCK, EXPANSION, MONEY, EXTRAVAGANCE, OBESITY, PLENTIFUL, FORTUNE, PHILOSOPHY, LONG JOURNEYS, RELIGION, NOBILITY, HIGH-MINDEDNESS, FRANKNESS, AND ANYTHING LARGE IN A PHYSICAL SENSE OR EXPANSIVE IN ANY MANNER.

This number, in picking winners, is considered fortunate.

IF THE TOTAL IS 4:

Number 4 is associated with the planet Uranus and with the zodiacal sign of Aquarius the Water Bearer.

Key words: ELECTRICITY, RESTRICTION, FRIENDS, WISHES, TELEVISION, AVIATION, MAGNETISM, GRAVITY, ASTROLOGY, STRENGTH, SQUARE, DETAILS, METHODS, FULFILLMENT, TEST, AND ANYTHING ASSOCIATED WITH FULFILLMENT OF WISHES BASED ON HARD WORK.

This number, in picking winners, is **not** as fortunate as some others.

IF THE TOTAL IS 5:

Number 5 is associated with the planet Mercury and with the zodiacal signs of Gemini the Twins and Virgo the Virgin.

Key words: INVESTIGATION, COMMUNICATION, MEMBERS OF THE OPPOSITE SEX, LOVE, ADVENTURE, CHANGE, TRAVEL, VARIETY, DETECTIVES, SHORT JOURNEYS, DISCRIMINATION. SERVANTS, JOB, BROTHERS AND SISTERS, AFFAIR OF THE HEART, MARRIAGE AND ANYTHING ASSOCIATED WITH CREATIVE ACTIVITY.

This number, in picking winners, is considered fortunate.

IF THE TOTAL IS 6:

Number 6 is associated with the planet Venus and with the zodiacal signs of Taurus the Bull and Libra the Scales.

Key words: HOME, LOVED ONES, FAMILY, CHANGE OF RESIDENCE, DOMESTICITY, VOICE, LUXURY, LAZINESS, COLLECTING, MONEY, JUSTICE, LEGAL CONTRACTS, HOBBIES ASSOCIATED WITH THE ACCUMULATION OF OBJECTS. SUCH AS COINS, STAMPS, PAINTINGS, ETC., TRANQUILITY, PEACE AND ANYTHING ASSOCIATED WITH HOME AND FAMILY, OR WITH THE VOICE AND SECURITY.

This number, in picking winners, is **not** as fortunate as some others.

IF THE TOTAL IS 7:

Number 7 is associated with the planet Neptune and the zodiacal sign of Pisces the Fish.

Key words: DECEPTION, PARTNERS, INSTITUTIONS SUCH AS PRISONS, HOSPI-

TALS, ORPHANAGES, E T C., ILLUSION, NON-REALITY, WATER, M O T I O N PICTURES, TELEVISION, AN "UNSEEN AUDIENCE," PSYCHIC PHENOMENA, MEDIUMS, EXTRA-SENSORY PERCEPTION, SPIRITUALISM, OR ANYTHING ASSOCIATED WITH INFLUENCES WHICH CAN BE FELT BUT NOT SEEN.

This number, in picking winners, is either **very good** or **unfortunate in the extreme**.

IF THE TOTAL IS 8:

Number 8 is associated with the planet Saturn and the zodiacal sign of Capricorn the Goat.

Key words: MONEY POWER, RESPONSIBILITY, COMMERCIAL S U C C E S S, MARRIAGE, SEX, CREATIVITY, CONCEPTION, PREGNANCY, STANDING IN THE COMMUNITY, AMBITION, ASPIRATIONS, AUTHORITY, THE PAST, BONES, AND ANYTHING ASSOCIATED WITH CAREER, DECAY OR BUSINESS.

This number, in picking winners, is considered fortunate.

IF THE TOTAL IS 9:

Number 9 is associated with the planet Mars and the zodiacal sign of Aries the Ram.

Key words: UNIVERSAL APPEAL, ADVERTISING, PUBLIC RELATIONS, PUBLISHING, NURSING, SYMPATHY, CONSIDERATION, FAME, RECOGNITION, HOSPITALS, PERSONALITY, WAR AND PEACE, AND ANYTHING ASSOCIATED WITH POETRY, SYMBOLISM, WORLD-WIDE PUBLICATIONS.

This number, in picking winners, is considered fortunate.

IF THE TOTAL IS 11:

Number 11 is associated with the planet Uranus and the zodiacal sign of Aquarius the Water Bearer.

Key words: INTUITION, OCCULT, TEACHER, WRITER, INSTRUCTOR, PREDICTION, HELP FROM FRIENDS, POWER, ADVENTURE, ENERGY FROM UNKNOWN SOURCES, SACRED, LIBERTY, BRAVERY, UNDERSTANDING, RELIGION, AND ANYTHING ASSOCIATED WITH PHILOSOPHY AND FAITH.

This number, in picking winners, is considered fortunate.

IF THE TOTAL IS 22:

Number 22 is associated with the planet Pluto and the zodiacal sign of Scorpio the Scorpion.

Key words: MASTER, BUILDER, BRILLIANCE, FUTURE, IDEALS, ALTRUISM, ORGANIZATION, COMMUNITY, MONEY OBTAINED FROM PARTNERS, EXPRESSION, MESSENGER, TEARING DOWN IN ORDER TO REBUILD, THINGS HIDDEN, AND ANYTHING ASSOCIATED WITH COMPLETION OR UTOPIA.

This number, in picking winners, is considered fortunate.

VARIATIONS

It might be asked why the subject is told to dial three numbers: why not one? why not four? or five? or any total?

The answer is that my research was based on a series of three digits. The experiments, thus far conducted with the Thought Dial, have been concerned with the series of three. This is not to say that another total might not be equally as effective. Perhaps, in some instances, the workings of the Thought Dial would be enhanced with a different series.

Thus, Sepharial, in discussing thoughts in relation to number, advocates a series of nine numbers, which are then reduced in the usual manner. And to which the number three is added. Sepharial also cites examples of other experts in these matters who take only one number—deriving their interpretation from that single digit.

It is my belief that, if working with the same subject, the operator of the Thought Dial might be well advised to **vary** his technique. Perhaps the subject is working the Thought Dial in a series of tests. Use the three-number method, vary it with the series of nine digits, with the number three added to the total. The Thought Dial, like thought itself, is fluid: it is not fixed. Nor is this text intended to be gospel.

The material here, in most instances, is put down as the result of experiments which proved fruitful. The important thing to remember is the Thought Dial is **merely an instrument throughtwhich the**

subconscious mind is permitted to express itself.

In continuous experiments with a subject, it might be advisable to vary methods of arriving at a total. The significant factor is the **total,** whether that total is arrived at by the dialing of three numbers, or one number, or nine numbers with the addition of three to the final answer.

Example: Operator has subject dial three numbers to obtain insight into his **subconscious thoughts.**

Subject is then requested to think of a **specific question,** and to once more dial three numbers.

The subject has yet another direct question. Once more he is instructed to dial three numbers.

Subject, at this point, has a question concerning a **lost article.** Operator requests that he dial **nine** numbers, which are added and reduced in the usual manner—except that number three is added to the total.

Subject, in asking still another direct question, once more is instructed to **dial three** numbers.

In conclusion, subject—in selecting "a winner"—is told to dial **one** number.

By this technique, the subject's interest is held. This is an important point to remember. Dr. Rhine, in his numerous experiments with ESP, concluded that **higher scores** resulted when the subject's interest was at a peak. As the interest waned, so did ESP scores.

Why this is so, I leave to others to determine.

FURTHER EXAMINATION

Man, as we have indicated, did not invent numbers: he **discovered** them. Indeed, before the advent of man, Nature apparently made use of number and symbol. In effect, man came along and learned to follow Nature's example.

I am now going to quote Lawrence Lipton, a poet and scholar of Venice, California. Lipton's work has appeared in numerous influential publications in this country and abroad: his opinions and essays —often of a controversial nature—are quoted and reprinted. His challenging concepts have appeared in **Life Magazine, Chicago Review, The Nation, The London Magazine, Arizona Quarterly** and **The Atlantic,** among other publications. He is the author of two novels and his **Rainbow at Midnight** was a Book Club for Poetry selection in 1955. Lipton's scholarly interests have included anthropology, linguistics, language origins, history, philosophy, literature and the sciences.

Commenting on the Thought Dial—and its use of symbols—Lipton states:

"I suspect that what you have here is a **mantram,** which is what the Buddhists would call it. A **mantram** is an object which, in itself, is a symbol, **something which sets off or triggers the numinous** experience of the individual, so that he becomes, for the moment, a receptor for whatever truth he is seeking. That truth may be a desire to understand the future or to relive the past. It may be a desire to understand the inner workings of his own psyche. It may be a desire to know whether he should **marry, or go into business for himself, or whatever** it is he is trying to do or understand. **The Thought Dial** becomes for him a **mantram** which triggers the mechanism. And it is as valid as the user or subject can make it. Any **mantram,** in this sense, is limited in its value to what the user or subject can make of it. All symbols are metaphors. And metaphors are interpreted by the individual within the scope of his own understanding."

Those are the words of Lawrence Lipton—and they are enlightening. He goes on to say:

"All views of the world and the universe are human-mental in concept. In order to communicate these concepts we use number and symbol. I suspect these symbols are **not** confined to human life. Animals use number and symbol. The bees, for example, are known to use a language which certainly consists of number and symbol. Writer Gerald Heard has written extensively of this—bees being able to communicate to each other regarding the location and sources of nectar supply. Bees are known to move to the left, right, up and down, a certain number of motions creating a map, enabling them to communicate with other bees in the hive. So, you see, symbols are not limited to man. The entire universe is alive, is articulate and communicates. The line between the numerology of crystals to the mathematics of Einstein is only a matter of degree."

Lipton, whose scholarship is respected among writers and intellectuals, continues:

"The whole universe is based upon number. This, of course, has been known for a long time. It was known to Pythagoras and others. Number is language. Language never had a beginning. It is as old as life is, at both ends of the scale—past and present. Communication implies symbol. The language of the chromosome, for example—I speak of it as a language because the communication which takes place between the cells and the growth apparatus in the single cell and the multiplying cell—is arranged very much as a script might be.

"Much of man's knowledge of number comes from the **Kabala**. The **Kabala**, historically, represents a rather late attempt to rediscover the mystery of numbers in relation to human conduct. The **Kabala**, if read with an eye to metaphor rather than to strict mathematics, can be understood. It is to be read in the same way Jung has re-read astrology and alchemy. Ultimately, all mathematical symbols are reducible to metaphor . . .

"The Kabala was passed on orally for a long time, going back perhaps to the Alexandrian Jews, who were influenced by the Hermetic teachings of the Greek gnostic and Neo-platonic cults. One of its principal sources is the **Zohar**, which the 13th century scholar Moses de Leon attributed to Simon ben Yochai, a great scholar of the 2nd century. The greatest influence of the Kabala, on both Jews and Christians, dates from the 7th century onwards in Europe, undergoing corruption from century to century as its meanings became clouded by ignorance and exploitation by charlatans."

Lipton concludes, by saying:

"In Hebrew legend, God created the world by **number**. He did this by means of an alphabet, which appeared in letters of fire above his crown. **Every letter has a number.** Hebrews, like Greeks, **use letters to denote number,** as well as alphabetical or phonetic sign.

"All symbols, including the symbols on the Thought Dial, have a relationship to our needs. Anything that exists in the universe, anything that is conceivable, has a past, present and future. In a real sense the past and present and future exist simultaneously. Every now and then some persons obtain an inkling of eternity. Animals appear to have the faculty of seeing the past, present and future as one. Some animals can predict weather and thus prepare themselves, for example, with a thick coat. The eye is formed in embryo before there is any need for sight. Does the embryo know it is going to need an eye when born?

"Yes, it appears that Nature has prepared a script, one that is built into each organism, making it prophetic, enabling it to see beyond the present and into the future. If this is true in Nature—objects appearing before their purpose has become a reality—then there is no reason why the human mind cannot also conceive of the future. If it is possible for a hedgehog, it is certainly possible for a human being."

Those are the comments of Lawrence. Lipton regarding the Thought Dial.

SOUND AND COLOR

Numbers, as symbols, are related to **sounds** and **colors** as well as to planets and thoughts.

Here, the numbers are being presented as they relate to sound and color. As Lipton declares, it is up to the user to get what he can from this relationship. Perhaps the **color** relationship will prove helpful in association with the section on **Picking Winners**. Or in relation to **Locating Lost Articles**. That, I leave to the individual. More experiment is required.

As for **sound,** perhaps some students will evolve a method of utilizing the Thought Dial to **depict names,** just as it now can be used to perceive zodiacal signs. This, of course, remains to be seen.

I present the Thought Dial symbols in relation to **sound** and **color** in the spirit of experiment. I will, as in all instances, be most anxious to hear from students regarding their experiments with this section.

NUMBER ONE:

Color: orange, gold.

Sound: A and I and the consonants M, D, T.

NUMBER TWO:

Color: green.

Sound: B, P, F, V.

NUMBER THREE:

Color: violet, purple.

Sound: related to all palatals, as Ch, J, and soft G.

NUMBER FOUR:
Color: gray, black and white (stripes).
Sound: C.

NUMBER FIVE:
Color: yellow, pink.
Sound: E, H, N.

NUMBER SIX:
Color: primrose, turquoise, pale blue.
Sound: O, U, W

NUMBER SEVEN:
Color: Lavender, lilac, heliotrope.
Sound: similar to 2: B ,P, F, V.

NUMBER EIGHT:
Color: indigo, dark blue, chocolate, black.
Sound: S, Sh, Z.

NUMBER NINE:
Color: red, scarlet, crimson.
Sound: K, hard G, R.

NUMBER ELEVEN:
Color: similar to 4: gray, black and white (stripes).
Sound: similar to 4: C.

NUMBER TWENTY-TWO:
Color: red and black.
Sound: S, K, G, R.

CONCLUSIONS

Admittedly, the title of this section is misleading. The late philosopher William James once said, in effect, that nothing is concluded that we might conclude from it. In a sense, this is true when we talk about the Thought Dial. It is a start, a spark that could break out into a flame: the purpose of this work is to provide that spark. It will be up to readers, to students, to those who experiment with the material we have provided here—it will be those persons who kindle the spark and create, finally, a rousing flame, the warmth that comes with greater knowledge.

As I say, I know the Thought Dial "works." I have tried, in these pages, to tell all I **consciously** know of this **mantram,** this device which, at present, clearly falls into the field of the **mantic** sciences. There are really no conclusions possible at this time. But the necessity of putting down what we **do** know seemed imperative: what will come of it, as I say, remains to be seen.

I know that **disciplined experiment** is required: the Thought Dial, in the current stage, can be compared to Benjamin Franklin putting a kite aloft in an electric storm. In itself, that act was meaningless. What it meant to the future, of course, was quite another matter.

It is my hope that men of the caliber of Drs. Rhine and Jung, and others, will conduct experiments with the Thought Dial, aided by the experiences and reports of readers of this work. When we deal with the language of symbols we are on such fertile ground that no real end, or "conclusion" is in sight. There is so much to try, to do, to read, to conclude!

Anais Nin, the writer of superb novels, talks of the **need** of symbols. A listener asks, "Why not say what you mean in the first place and thus eliminate symbols?" She replies that often the "truth" is too terrible to bear, and only through the use of the symbol can the conscious mind comprehend what is buried deep, in the subconscious or secret or hidden mind.

She is borne out by others, in various fields of endeavor. Leo Stalnaker, in his excellent **Mystic Symbolism in Bible Numerals,*** declares: "The origin of the science of symbols is lost in the maze of early antiquity. Though the beginning is not known, it doubtless connects itself with the cradle of humanity, and the science comes down to us from an age when only a few could read or write. Man's earliest instruction was by symbols. A thing to be symbolic must really mean something, and must, in its nature, be a proper, adequate or fitting sign or token of something."

Stalnaker, like Lawrence Lipton, points out that, "The importance of numerical symbolism to the ancients perhaps arose from the fact that the letters of the Hebrew language were originally numerals, and the entire Bible being composed of different groups or combinations of Hebrew letters, it came to be the common belief that the true meaning or proper interpretation of difficult passages of Scripture could best be ascertained or reached only by resorting to the numerical value of those letters."

Man's way of **communicating,** his language, his alphabet, the sounds and words he utters, are **symbols,** probably all relating to number. Through use of the Thought Dial, the subconscious is able to **communicate** with our conscious minds, much in the manner that dream symbols can enlighten us.

*C & R Anthony, Inc., Publishers, New York (1956)

The literature available is enormous, from the Bible to the most modern of scientific texts. I will not—this, I admit, could be an error—attempt to provide a list of recommended reading. I know I would, through ignorance or carelessness, neglect to mention pertinent material.

What I hope to do, from time to time, is to issue supplemental material to be utilized in connection with the Thought Dial. The material will be based on future experience (experiment), both on a personal level and from reports obtained from readers —plus additional "reading" research.

Kurt Seligmann, in his remarkable **The History of Magic*** (originally published under the title, **The Mirror of Magic**) states, "Without pretense to original scholarship, my investigation has been guided by such scholarly works as those of . . ."

In a way, that is what I wish to say: no pretense is being made that **Thought Dial** falls into the category of "scientific" or "scholarly" work. But I have been guided by the highest motives and by great works and scholars. If the reader was by my side, in my study, I would reel off a list of recommended reading. This, perhaps, will follow in supplemental material. My "intuitive intellect" tells me it is not in place here, for the material ranges from the volumes of writers Henry Miller and Gertrude Stein, to those of Nostradamus, the interpreters of the **Kabala,** to the writings of Sepharial, Isidore Kozminsky, Seligmann, Jung, Cheiro, Evangeline Adams, Freud, Ariel Yvonne Taylor, Dr. Alexander Cannon, Florence Campbell, Stalnaker, Clifford Cheasley, Alfred Still, Clark E. Moustakas, Karen Horney, Constance Reid, Tobey, Grant Lewi, Manly Palmer Hall, Charles Fort, Rhine, William James, Marc Edmund Jones, Lilly, Ptolemy, Dr. Gustaf Stromberg, Mrs. L. Dow Balliett, Lawrence Lipton, Aldous Huxley, Waldo Frank, Julia Seaton

*Pantheon Books. New York (1948)

. . . and the list could be extended indefinitely, for it includes such sources as the Bible and the **Kabala** and the **Zohar** and so on, right up to the present: the language of **thought** and **symbol** is universal, a part of Nature, of life itself.

As I have said, before his death Thomas Alva Edison was reported to be engrossed in the possibility of a "telephone between worlds," a physical device which, he speculated, would eventually make it possible for persons living to communicate with those who had met bodily death. His theory, like the theories of Dr. Stromberg, Sir Oliver Lodge, Sir Arthur Conan Doyle and others, was that the human personality or memory or "spirit" survived after bodily death. There could be an analogy between Edison's "telephone between worlds" and the Thought Dial.

The subconscious, or "inner mind," may be in contact with whatever it is in man that survives. I do not know or claim to understand the subconscious. Like so many other things in our language, it represents a symbol—to me it is a convenient way of giving a "name" to the force that is tapped through utilization of the Thought Dial.

I defer my conclusion.

I await further word—from you.

INTRODUCTION TO SECOND EDITION

BY CARL PAYNE TOBEY

A great many people are unable to adjust their subjective world to the objective world. Because of the condition of the subjective world, they are seldom able to truly explore the reality of the objective world. We have a lot of such persons in mental institutions. We have far more outside of mental institutions. Some of them may be housewives. Others are teaching in schools and universities. The writer met such a teacher the other night. It is unfortunate that under our educational system such people are often given the responsibility of handling our young, when they should be receiving treatment. The writer has no desire to fool himself, and when he was first confronted with the *Thought Dial,* he was on guard against this very thing. Over a period of years, it always worked for the writer. Would it work for others? Would it work for everybody or just for some people? This is not an easy thing to find out. We can't answer for everybody, because we don't know everybody, and we can't test everybody. In writing the introduction to the first edition of the *Thought Dial,* the writer stated his honest views as best he could. He stated that the *Thought Dial* had worked for him and that he didn't know why.

After publication of the first edition, the writer talked 300 persons into buying and trying out the

Thought Dial, guaranteeing the return of anyone's money who didn't think it was worth the price after trying it out. In each case, the individual was asked to report back if it DID NOT work for him or for her. Many reports came back. It is a rather astonishing thing to realize that out of 300 people, not one person came back and said, "I have tried the *Thought Dial* out. It completely failed to work for me."

Frankly, I was almost certain that some person would come back and say something along those lines. I felt positive that we would find someone for whom the *Thought Dial* had no value. You find exceptions to most rules. Even in physics, we have to keep adjusting our theories and conception of things. This is not proof that there is not someone for whom the *Thought Dial* does not work. Not until we know more about the human mind will we know.

Some of these three hundred people who purchased the *Thought Dial* on the writer's suggestion were scientists, persons well educated and well trained in accurately observing facts. These were the first people to respond, and they all told us that the *Thought Dial* worked for them. They didn't know why, but they were highly amused that it did. Two psychiatrists reported back. They are qualified persons to investigate such a phenomenon as the *Thought Dial.* Their reaction was the same, "It really does work!"

One psychologist, not a member of the above group, has developed a technique where the *Thought Dial* is employed to further probe the subconscious as a means to clearing or curing the patient. In this technique, the patient is asked to respond to certain words with numbers, which enables the psychologist to understand what ideas and conceptions are wrongly identified with each other in the subconscious.

The truth is always within yourself if you could but bring it out, but there are a lot of things other than the truth that are also hidden in your subconscious. There is a very ancient saying that first thoughts are best. This has some basis in fact, and it has been proved in extra-sensory perception tests that most people will be likely to guess best the first time. The second guess is not as valuable as the first, and there is a greater probability of the first guess being right. There may be some connection. The *Thought Dial* is a way of guessing when you are unconscious of doing so. You ask for numbers, and your subconscious tosses them up from somewhere. They come up in such a way that they have value *when applied to the Thought Dial*. It is a strange phenomenon, but most interesting. It stimulates one's curiosity, and all progress in the world has occurred because someone got curious. Otherwise, life would probably develop into a dull routine. The *Thought Dial* will help keep life from becoming a monotonous routine. It's fun, but it's a lot more than that, too. It holds the answer to some of the many mysteries of the mind. Get curious yourself and do a little exploring. Try it out on your friends. Help them with their problems. Be a very careful observer. See whether you can find a case where it doesn't work, and if you do, report the case with great care. The nearest thing the writer had to a negative report was one person who wrote, "It doesn't get into my subconscious. *It tells me exactly what I'm thinking about consciously,* and it does it all the time." Well, even that is rather odd!

If you are original, you probably have some ideas of your own about these things. Experiment with them and see what you can find out. A teen-ager had been listening to conversations about the *Thought Dial*. He and a companion became interested. They talked about it to a third teen-ager who was more than skeptical.

"Try it out and see," one of the boys said. "Ask it a question."

The skeptical lad began dialing. He wanted a specific *yes* or *no* answer to a question. The answer came up, *"Yes!"* The boy said nothing but looked puzzled.

"What was your question?" one of the boys impatiently asked.

The lad replied, "Does this thing work?"

C.P.T.

UP TO NOW

In a short space of time, *Thought Dial* is enlarged in this second edition. Response has been more than gratifying. It is a fond hope that *Thought Dial* will continue to grow with each edition. This depends, to a great extent, upon you, the reader—reports on your experiments and experiences with *TD* help add dimension, help us arrive at conclusions and help toward the goal of truth. With each new edition, supplemental material — the added material comprising the new edition — will be issued separately so that those working with *TD* can keep up to date on latest findings, experiments, suggestions, conclusions, etc.

The remarkable thing about *TD* concerns not only its reception by purchasers, but the very wonderful treatment received through the public communications media: newspapers, radio, television. Good reception in these areas help the entire field of new thought, including astrology. This is no small matter. These areas have been, and still are, riddled with academic prejudice: doors are constantly closed and kept shut tight by the orthodoxy. When public opinion changes, only then will the power of the orthodoxy sway, at least a little, in favor of persons working on the "outside," persons interested in astrology, numerology, hand analysis, extra-sensory perception, psychic phenomena, abstract science, etc. Academic prejudice is a very real threat: it spills over poisonous juices and attempts to destroy truth. Examination of numerous text books will readily show how this kind of poison has attempted to twist and alter history itself — i.e., Paracelsus *couldn't* have been an astrologer! Pythagoras didn't *really* believe in numerology; Nostradamus never really *used* astrology! Jung isn't *serious* about astrology! No great astronomer *accepted* astrology! Mathematicians reject the *symbolism* of numbers! And on and on and on . . . *including dictionary definitions which are no longer definitions but editorial comments* ("astrology a pseudoscience . . .").

But the pendulum is swinging over, slowly but surely. This publication—its reception—helps make that point clear.

*   *   *

Now, what are we basically stating? We are saying, with all the firmness at our command, that numbers are *subjective* as well as objective. We are saying that numbers have meaning and language and the power of communication, as alphabets do and as letters in alphabets possess that same power. We are declaring that numbers, like music, represent a *universal language*. We are saying that *thoughts,* intangible in themselves, can be reduced to number and thus made tangible.

True, the number is a symbol, not a literal statement. But to be able to obtain a *visual symbol* of such a thing as a *thought* is of paramount value, a giant step in progress, an exciting one, a tremendous adventure, the brink of enlightenment.

The actual *dial* of the *Thought Dial* is but a *mantram,* an instrument, just as the crystal ball is to the crystal gazer or the bowl of water is to some clairvoyants. It would be just as practical, perhaps, for a person to name numbers or select them in any fashion, eliminating the dial. The dial of *Thought Dial* is a convenience. It is a good convenience. It serves a purpose. But the experienced practitioner needn't be concerned with carrying a dial on his person. He can just as well have his subject write number selections or state them orally.

The principles, illustrations and examples provided in the first edition have held up. Experience is the one ingredient which improves the practitioner. *Use* of the *TD* is a necessity. Practice in *interpretation* of the numbers brings with it added skill. Just as an astrologer becomes skilled at interpreting planetary positions and aspects in a horoscope, so does the *user* of the *TD* gain added skill through numerous experiments. The basis, the principles are there: how well they are *utilized* depends upon the determination and talent of the individual operator. A good analogy, of course, is the doctor who becomes an excellent diagnostician. The same symptoms are available to all doctors, but relatively few medical men become outstanding diagnosticians.

The fact that *TD works* is the important factor. It works because of reasons outlined in the first edition, or at least because of *some* of those reasons. All of the answers, as yet, are not known. To be successful in using the information contained here about *thoughts* and *numbers* it is important to *grasp basic meanings*. Afterwards, the interpretations can be filled out, the "filling" process coming with practice, experiment, experience, skill.

Now, what is meant by the *grasping* of these meanings? To this date, the best example was forthcoming from *Dorothy Lyon,* of Los Angeles. She reports that "my first three trials gave me amazingly appropriate answers."

Miss Lyon puts it well: "appropriate answers." *TD* takes the intangible or the unseen and permits us to "have a look," to examine something which contains substance and solidity (numbers). Miss Lyon tells of her first three trials. The initial one concerned retirement. Her *TD* total was 9.

The second was a question about a lady who felt she was not appreciated by her husband—whether or or not to leave him. The total was 4.

The third trial concerned a foot disorder. The total was 7.

I can recall, more than ten years ago, visiting Carl Payne Tobey, who was then confined to a hospital in New York. He was suffering a foot disorder. We were discussing the principles of *TD*. Carl gave three numbers. The total was 7. Number 7 is associated with Neptune. That planet, according to *TD* principles, is in turn related to the zodiacal sign of Pisces. That sign rules the feet. Number 7 is indeed "appropriate" in connection with Miss Lyon's third trial!

Number 7, of course, in another question or *thought,* might relate to an individual born under Pisces or its opposite sign, Virgo.

Just as the twelve houses of a horoscope conceivably could cover every department of life, so the number totals of *TD* might be associated or analogous to any question or thought.

It might be well, at this point, to relate the totals to various bodily parts:

ONE—Back and Heart.

TWO—Stomach, Breasts.

110

THREE—Thighs.

FOUR—Heart, Back, Stomach.

FIVE—Arms, Hands, Kidneys.

SIX—Neck, Throat, Lumbar Regions.

SEVEN—Feet.

EIGHT—Knees.

NINE—Head, Face.

ELEVEN—Legs, Ankles, Teeth, Circulation.

TWENTY-TWO—Genitals.

In the first trial mentioned by Miss Lyon, the number 9 came up in a question relating to retirement. For a person who "grasps" the principles, this is an obvious total. Number 9, of course, relates to finish, completion, the end of one phase of activity in preparation for another.

In her second example, Miss Lyon mentions the word "unappreciated" in connection with a woman who is pondering the state of her marriage. The total is 4. This is a natural total for such a thought or question, the number 4 being a symbol of restriction, of being "hemmed in" to a stifling degree. Number 4 brings a need for freedom or a feeling for freedom because, at least temporarily, it is being denied.

TD consistently provides these "appropriate" symbols. It remains for each of us to strive for better understanding and interpretation of these totals. The sky is the limit with the principles we have evolved here.

*   *   *

Boxing promoter Tom Hurst, of Manchester, England, experienced success with the *Locating Lost Articles* section of *TD*. Surprisingly, so did numerous other persons. "Surprisingly," because this was one of the more speculative sections or chapters. Mr. Hurst reports, "But the thing is amazing—even in little, silly things such as a length of sorbo rubber, ½ inches by ¼ inches and 8 feet long. It was looked for a dozen times. And more for a joke than anything, we tried the Dial. IN TWO MINUTES we had the rubber . . ."

Mrs. Al Downs, of Los Angeles, received a telephone call from a friend in distress. She had lost something. Mrs. Downs asked her for three numbers. She then told her in which direction to look for the lost object. In a short time, the friend called again: she had found what she was looking for—and accused Mrs. Downs of being clairvoyant!

*   *   *

A professional astrologer in San Antonio, Texas, reports as follows: "I think I shall tell you at this point one of the main features in successful use of *Thought Dial*. It is this: I have a very good mail order business, so I do this with each *unopened* (repeat, *unopened and unread!)* letter from a client:—I place the letter (asking for astrological services) *behind* the *Thought Dial* (pressing against back of the Dial) then I concentrate. The result: practically *every* time (almost unfailingly) the subject's *birth sign* or *ascendant* is dialed!"

The above represents application of the theory that the *TD* symbols are analogous or symbolic of the birth sign, as explained in the first edition, at the beginning of the section titled, *Direct Questions Answered*.

*   *   *

Communications media reception to *TD* was mentioned earlier. Thanks are due to Ben Hunter, of radio station *KFI,* Los Angeles, to George Fisher, of *KHJ,* Los Angeles, and to numerous others, including James Crenshaw, of the *Los Angeles Herald & Express.* His review of *TD* is reproduced here because it appeared in a major, daily metropolitan newspaper and is thus of some historic importance. Also, users of *TD* might like to know of the reactions of a trained seeker-of-facts, a professional reporter. Here is Mr. Crenshaw's brief review, under the heading, *THOUGHT DIAL INTRIGUING,* as it appeared on July 7, 1958:

"In this modern age of subliminal advertising, psycho-somatic illness and hypno-therapy, the advent of new gimmicks for probing the subconscious is bound to be expected.

"Writer Sydney Omarr has hit on one that is both fascinating and unique. After years of experimentation and research by Omarr, Llewellyn Publications of Los Angeles, long-time publishers of astrological literature, have brought out his THOUGHT DIAL, a book-plus-gadget combination designed to permit the individual to probe his own subconscious and come up with some helpful answers.

"Much of the small book is concerned with theoretical explanations of why the gadget appears to work. Behind it is the recognized principle that numbers are symbols with an intrinsic meaning which the subconscious can grasp.

"Since the subconscious, according to Omarr, has been shown by extra-sensory experiments to have extraordinary powers of awareness in areas far beyond the conscious mind, the number-symbols can be used to tap this reservoir."

113

An unusual communication was received from Lucille Wallenborn, of Bell Gardens, California. She declared that *TD* seemed only to reiterate "the problem—or give a number which corresponds to what I am consciously thinking, hoping, or fearing." This woman, in other words, finds that the *TD* tells what is *consciously* on her mind, but does not probe deeper or provide special insight. In itself, this is interesting and certainly worthy of consideration. The theory behind *TD* is that we are *aware* of the right answers, but very often those answers are buried deep in the subconscious, and if the answers are unpleasant, the censor or conscious mind is apt to distort them by the time they appear at the surface. Miss Wallenborn's experience seems to slightly contradict this theory, although her experience in general is an encouraging one for the student—for it provides fuel for thought and further experiment.

*   *   *

Kathleen F. Barnes, of Detroit, Michigan, presents what she terms "certain startling facts regarding my experience with *Thought Dial* . . ." She had been a student of Carl Payne Tobey's course in astrology: it was through Tobey that she came into possession of *TD*. She explains that she seems to have a natural distaste for mathematics, so it was with some surprise that she found herself investigating "certain strange designs involving digits and numbers." At first, she states, she was merely intrigued. But later, "I was engaged in a most diligent search for clues that would give this design some astrological meaning. Having found 'the key' I was off in search of 'the lock' to which it belonged. It turned out that 'the key' fit into an almost uncanny system of investigating the structure of a chart and the life belonging to it."

Miss Barnes goes on to report: "Naturally, this fascinated me, but because I was doubtful of my ability to get the idea across successfully to Mr. Toby (it's hard to explain the details), I developed a strange impression of having a lion by the tail and did not dare to let go, so I merely continued to use the formula in experimenting with charts.

"I am not a professional astrologer—at least not yet. Then *Thought Dial* arrived. At first I was disappointed, and then exceedingly annoyed with it because it seemed to clutter up my lovely number system. However, there was something about my annoyance which called for an explanation, and as is customary, when my mind goes wandering, something unusual turned up. SOME-THING about this *Thought Dial* produced a sense of familiarity. I set out to discover what it was, and holy! purple!! Shades of JUPITER!! it turns out that the system incorporated into *Thought Dial* paralleled my 'mantric' number system, which is based emphatically on Mr. Tobey's planetary number assignment. They both operate by the same principle. Though it was a little difficult to track down this similarity . . . it eventually became obvious that the numbers assigned to houses and planets by Mr. Tobey were accurate and your interpretation, instead of upsetting them, merely proved their accuracy. *Thought Dial* becomes an expression of the dynamics stressed in any Natal or Solar chart PLUS the mathematical design of the transits."

Miss Barnes concludes by saying, "For me, this links *TD* with Mr. Tobey's work in a most harmonious way. By allowing for the changes effected by TIME and MOTION, the total and complete design is indicated by the *TD*. My 'mantric system' has its source in incontrovertible facts. The cycles incorporated as parts of a design and 'dialed' by the astrologer in sets of three, total up to a whole number that explains the combined dynamics and, at the same time, highlights any particular aspect which contributes to the dynamic in motion.

"The whole effect is somewhat uncanny because the chart seems to live and breathe, and to tell you the truth, I felt a little bit afraid of it until I encountered *TD* because it is a confirmation of the 'mantric system' which was, to say the least, most electrifying.

"I acknowledge *TD* as the 'Geiger Counter' of the astrological realm."

So, here we have an example of a student who had evolved her own numerical system, combining it with principles of astrology, in this case Mr. Tobey's course. She states that her system "worked." Then, along came *TD* and her *own system* suddenly basked in the light of greater clarity.

*   *   *

At least two psychiatrists, one medical doctor who is not a psychiatrist, and one consulting psychologist, now make use of *TD* or apply its principles. These responses and results are being provided in this second edition because, though in themselves they may not prove or disprove a thing, the *combination* may help us toward greater understanding of what we have here, or toward eventual uses in specific areas of life. A little later in this edition, a new *dimension* of *TD* will be revealed. This dimension, it is felt, reprsents perhaps a new, important use of *TD*. It is a psychological technique which the author staunchly believes will—in the not-too-distant-future—be integrated into numerous areas of psychological testing. It is an exciting, vital development and one of the outstanding reasons for an *enlarged* edition. More of this a little later.

For now, let us continue with reactions and responses, the reports of experiences encountered by users of *TD*. L. D. Wittkower, Sr., of Dallas, Texas, reports, "So far *TD* has proven so accurate it is amazing. I have never experienced anything like it."

John R. Hester, of Charlotte, North Carolina, comments, "I recently received my *TD* and it is literally *astounding!* It got me interested in numerology, which I find supplements my interest in astrology and the other esoteric branches. The horary astrology charts that I set up to seek answers to various questions used to keep me in a state of chronic frustration, due to the myriad varieties and necessity for skillful correlation of so many factors—a chart seldom gave a clear answer. *TD* has circumvented this in an indescribably satisfying way. Please be sure to issue periodical supplements as a sort of clearing medium for the experiences and suggestions of *TD* users."

W. R. Timoney, of Pasadena, California, a valuable worker and contributor of findings to the *Institute of Abstract Science,* in Tucson, Arizona, states, "I get the impression . . . that you lean on authority to too great an extent. It is when you get away from authorities that you are best. One of the best uses of external evidence you make in the entire book is in the section, *PICKING WINNERS.* You quote Matt Weinstock, of the *Los Angeles Mirror News,* to give some details. You fill in with some more details. You describe Ben Hunter's experiment, the outcome, and you analyze the procedure. This is first rate, scientific reportage. But in many places you try to tie astrology and the *TD* together. Maybe they are a part of the same whole; maybe not. Your arguments are not convincing. The *TD* is a very personal thing. It is analogous to a telephone line between the conscious and subconscious. Astrology is somewhat impersonal. It is analogous to a weather map of conditions surrounding the entire mind —conscious, subconscious, censor, etc. Because you use the symbols of astrology, you should not conclude that you use the principles. That may or may not be so. I happen to think you are much closer to the truth when you consider the *TD* as some kind of mantram."

Robert J. Trolan, of Indianapolis, Indiana, who is a "name analyst" and "Tarotologist," dispatches a lengthy communication which, though on the whole disparages *TD,* also contains much thought. Mr. Trolan opens by stating he pursued *TD* with an open mind and avid interest. "I experimented with it and gave it a good deal of thought for about eight hours. My wife, who also knows a good deal about the 'Tarot' through 15 years of association with me and my work, also examined your work quite closely! Upon both completing our checking of same, we were of virtually the same opinion, 'It is a marvelous idea and shows real ingenuity!' However, we also agreed that the last word, 'INGENUITY,' is exactly the only fault we both could find with *Thought Dial.*

" 'Ingenuity' is generally defined as (1) Cleverness in inventing; ingeniousness; (2) cleverness of design or construction; as ingenuity of plot; with syn.—Inventiveness and Originality".

Mr. Trolan goes on to explain his reaction: "We believe that, like hundreds of other authors we have read and, with a few exceptions, like so many modern and 'so-called experts' on symbology, both yourself and Mr. Tobey have succumbed to the same error that has plagued both our esoteric and exoteric sciences for the last several thousands of years! That is to inject their own 'ingenuity, cleverness, and inventiveness,' to take, as it were, 'fallacious license' with the symbology handed down to us by our mentors and superiors, the most ancient of 'Ancients.' The most astounding lack of disparity noticed in your work, is your almost studious avoidance of mention of the 'Sacred Tarot of Egypt,' or mention of men like Eliphas Levi, Elbert Benjamine (C. C. Zain), Max Heindel, John H. Dequer, and the sincere, but incomplete, St. Germain."

Mr. Trolan explains why, although he agrees with some of the text compromising the first edition, he disagrees with other facets of *TD*. He then closes by stating, "In closing, may I please again compliment you on your extraordinary accomplishment and upon the fact that your basic idea is sound. My only regret is that you could have the temerity to tamper with . . . mathematical verities and immutable certainties, just as Pythagoras did long before you, thereby coming up with a hybrid thing called numerology, which is here and there correct and mostly horribly incorrect. I am glad I have *TD* as it is of great interest to me, although it only serves to prove either how right you are and how wrong I am . . . or vice-versa."

*   *   *

From Josephine L. Whitbeck, of St. Helena, California, this communication: "My neighbor, Gordon Jackson, lent me his *TD*. When I had read enough to see what it was about, I tried the *Subconscious Thoughts* section, came out with a 6, and some advice on a problem of long standing, which applied very well Then I tried the *Yes and No* with the question, 'Shall I buy a *TD?*' Total was 1 (Yes-Definite). This pleased me. If it had been No, I think I would have got one anyway . . ."

*   *   *

I want to take this opportunity, now, to call attention to wonderful reaction and cooperation from one in the academic world. He is Dr. Hugo Norden, professor of the Theory of Music, at Boston University. After receiving his copy of *TD,* Dr. Norden began a correspondence with the author which, ultimately, will benefit all. Dr. Norden, on September 9, 1958, wrote:

"I have been spending some time with your *TD* and the accompanying book. Your mention of the possibilities of subconscious use of numbers interests me. Some musical works by Bach come to mind:

> *Passacaglia in C minor* — 21 sections, but so arranged as to bring in 4 overlapping, 11-section units.

> *Sinfonia No. 1* — 21-measure form, featuring 9 in a great many ways.

> *Sinfonia No. 3* — 25-measure form, featuring 4 overlapping, 7-measure units.

"This list could, of course, be continued indefinitely. But these three show a system.

"Now comes the question that every student asks: is this organization of ideas deliberate or does it 'just happen?' Personally, I am inclined to believe it was conscious up to a point, but that at a point that *cannot* be determined by analysis, the mechanism took over and developed features that were never planned nor intended by the composer."

Dr. Norden goes on to say: "In my work I have gradually become aware of something that is undoubtedly 'old stuff' to you; namely, that numbers operate in two ways:

> (1) as organizational numbers, as in the Bach Sinfonia No. 1 where the 21-measure form is divided into 13 plus 8 measures by a very

120

conspicuous division, and

(2) as 'essence' numbers arising out of the organization numbers, as in the case of 9 functioning within the 8:13:21 form.

Curiously enough, 7, 9 and 11 are most often 'essence' numbers, and not often organizational numbers."

In reply to Dr. Norden's comments, the following note was sent by the author, reproduced here for possible use or comment by the reader:

"I agree emphatically that certain stages or phases are 'planned' and after that the subconscious takes over and the organizational numbers take a back seat to what you term the 'essence' numbers.

"Numbers, of course, are inter-changeable with letters: the vowels are 'essence' or emotional while the consonants are apt to be organizational or utilitarian.

"Here is an experiment I wish you would try: take a composition or work and think about it and then give three spontaneous numbers. Total the result. Think of how certain works would affect certain of your students. Put down the total you think would represent the student's attitude or thoughts toward that work or composition or composer. Then, actually ask the student to think and select the numbers. See how close you come to guessing his total. Or, see if his total does not reveal more to you about the particular student, or that work, than you previously knew . . ."

Dr. Norden is continuing to experiment and to contribute and to make valued suggestions.

* * *

Charles A. Jayne, Jr., chairman of *Astrological*

Research Associates, New York, and editorial director of *In Search,* an international astrological quarterly, refers to *TD* as "amazing," and explains, "I say 'amazing' since only the night before last Dr. —————— sat in our living room and raved about it. He is a psychiatrist and has been testing *TD* for some time. He states that it is really uncanny. Please do not use his name . . ."

The psychiatrist mentioned (whose name we are not at liberty to reveal) by Mr. Jayne is not the only one who is utilizing the principles of *TD* in his work. We will go into this in our next section, *A New Dimension.*

Leading up to that area, let me now quote from a letter by Harry Redl, a brilliant San Francisco photographer:

"I don't know too much about the principle of *TD* but it instantly reminded me of a method used by the late Dr. Wilhelm Stekel, of Vienna, who was a student of Freud along with Jung.

"Dr. Stekel, upon reaching an impasse with an inhibited patient, would ask the patient to *name any three numbers that came to his mind.*

"Stekel's interpretation of the numbers was based not on metaphysical or magical considerations, but rather on direct symbolism.

"As I recall, the number 1 would represent the penis, number 3 would symbolize the male genitals with testicles, while number 5 was the human hand, and so on.

"Dr. Stekel also requested, from his patient, the birthdates of relatives, durations of relationships, and the age of the patient at the time of trauma occurrences . . ."

Mention of Dr. Stekel's experiment is, without doubt, both interesting and exciting. It reveals, among other things, that others (or at least one outstanding psychiatrist) have *perceived* the possibility of using numbers to probe the secrets of the mind. I am not familiar with Dr. Stekel's work. If other readers are, I would be most interested in hearing from them. Particularly, I would like to know in which volume of his work Dr. Stekel tells of his experience and experiments with numbers. Mr. Redl states that he read this volume in Vienna, but is sure that it has been translated into English. Interestingly, Dr. Stekel (according to Redl) associates number 5 with the hands, which would be in complete harmony with *TD*.

Let us now approach a new dimension of *Thought Dial.*

A NEW DIMENSION

There is no question about the most significant development in connection with *TD*. This development opens a new dimension and presents us with enormous possibilities. Just how far we can go, or where this new development eventually will lead, is a question to be answered by the future.

Let me open by quoting Dr. Bernard Cosneck, of Los Angeles, a consulting psychologist of 25 years experience. He states, "Sydney Omarr's instantaneous number selection is a valid personality test. It makes it possible for the person to bypass the false leads of the conscious mind and get to the subconscious mind where authentic information is stored."

Dr. Cosneck refers to the *TD* technique when he talks about "instantaneous number selection." He observed my experiments and work with *TD* principles and arrived at his above, quoted conclusion.

As readers know, the first edition was concerned—on the whole—with subconscious thoughts and specific questions. Our new dimension opens the door to interpretation of *direct* and *abstract* thoughts, ideas, associations. A close analogy would be the well-known word association test, whereby an individual is given a word, such as *door,* and asked to reel off a number of other words which come to mind when he thinks of *door.* Our *TD* varies in that the subject looks at or thinks of a word, such as *love,* and selects three numbers. The numbers, as in previous utilization of *TD,* are totalled and reduced to a single digit between 1 and 9, with the exceptions of 11 and 22, the only double numbers retained as final totals.

The implications here, the possibilities, are limitless. We are able to probe the subconscious in connection with such *abstracts* as LOVE, HATE, BEAUTY, DESPAIR, and in association with such *specifics* as SEX, MONEY, WORK, MARRIAGE, MOTHER, FATHER, etc.

Here is a sample test I devised, which was actually applied to a patient by a practicing psychologist, and reportedly with great success. Subsequently, other professionals — psychiatrists and medical hypnotists — utilized similar tests with encouraging results.

The patient will be called Mr. X. No mention was made to him of an actual "Thought Dial." He was told simply to look at the words given below, and to place three numbers beside each word. He was also instructed to first relax and to write down any three numbers (as a subject would do in the *Subconscious Thoughts* section).

Mr. X first wrote 9, 11 and 3, for a total of 23 or 5.

He was then confronted with the following words:

SAFETY

SEX

LOVE

JEALOUSY

HEIGHT

INFERIORITY

HANDSOME

MONEY

WORK

GIRL

SISTER-IN-LAW

AMERICA

SELF-CONFIDENCE

CHILDREN

MATURITY

MARRIAGE

COUSIN

MOTHER

DOCTOR

Mr. X, the patient or subject, then proceeded to place three numbers beside each of the words, with this result and the following totals:

SAFETY: 10, 203, 1. (totals 214 or 7)

SEX: 701, 12, 19. (totals 732 or 3)

LOVE: 21, 17, 23. (totals 61 or 7)

JEALOUSY: 26, 32, 35. (totals 93 or 3)

HEIGHT: 6, 11, 4. (totals 21 or 3)

INFERIORITY: 3, 7, 11. (totals 21 or 3)

HANDSOME: 22, 6, 36. (totals 64 or 1)

MONEY: 27, 32, 712. (totals 771 or 6)

WORK: 420, 56, 80. (totals 556 or 7)

GIRL: 19, 24, 20. (totals 63 or 9)

SISTER-IN-LAW: 40, 47, 50. (totals 137 or 11)

AMERICA: 71, 82, 95. (totals 248 or 5)

SELF-CONFIDENCE: 200, 4, 80. (totals 284 or 5)

CHILDREN: 2, 4, 7. (totals 13 or 4)

MATURITY: 31, 38, 20. (totals 89 or 8)

MARRIAGE: 10, 87, 23. (totals 120 or 3)

COUSIN: 30, 29, 17. (totals 76 or 4)

MOTHER: 58, 48, 39. (totals 145 or 1)

DOCTOR: 56, 48, 39. (totals 143 or 8)

It must be remembered that the subject, in this example, was *not* dialing, but merely giving spontaneous numbers in connection with the words in question. The subject had no idea what the test would reveal. The actual *Thought Dial* could just as well be used, but since a doctor was conducting the test—it was felt the atmosphere should be kept "clinical," that a *TD* might arouse suspicion, fear, or even worse, boil up academic prejudice within the patient. Use of the *TD* would have eliminated the large, double and triple numbers, thus simplifying the process of addition, if nothing else. However, what counts is the end result, the totals, not by which method the totals were forthcoming.

Now, if we will but think, the enormous potential of such a process becomes evident. Here, the analyst (or *TD* operator) is able to by-pass the conscious mind and *probe the subconscious* in connection with such factors as INFERIORITY, JEALOUSY, SEX and so on.

Let us now examine our subject's totals and draw some conclusions *based on the principles of TD*. First, his three numbers, given without reference to a word—9, 11, 3 (totals 23 or 5)—tells us he is (refer to number 5 in *Subconscious Thoughts* and other sections) concerned with relations with members of the opposite sex, with the possibility of marriage, with self-expression, with creativity; he wants to give of himself, make his mark, he is bursting with efforts toward self-expression. That is a beginning. It represents what is of concern to the subject. Here we are on "traditional" ground, or ground that is familiar through previous efforts with *TD*. It provides a starting point. We are not elaborating: the student who has come this far is able to "grasp principles." So, let us now see what our subject reveals when he places numbers beside the word SEX.

The 3 total, as our lessons in the first edition have taught us, represents a scattering of forces, confusion—nothing certain here or mature. Sex, for our subject, equals 3, giving light to a basic attitude of general confusion and anticipation. We note, also, that JEALOUSY totals 3.

Now we once more are *grasping principles*. Through our *TD* technique we are discovering *subconscious associations* in connection with our subject. We know that sex, for him, is 3: we now also have discerned that jealousy similarly totals 3. Jealousy and sex are tied tightly together in his subconscious thoughts, though he *may not consciously* admit or even be aware of this fact.

Other 3 totals include HEIGHT, INFERIORITY and MARRIAGE. In all, we have, under the 3 total SEX, JEALOUSY, HEIGHT, INFERIORITY and MARRIAGE.

These have been numerically or mathematically

grouped through our *TD* technique and thus we have entered *a new psychological dimension.* We have by-passed hypnosis and endless hours of questioning and endless statistical applications through *TD.* This is not, repeat *not* to advocate that statistical application or hypnosis or more orthodox forms be eliminated—what we *are* offering represents *an added psychological tool,* to be utilized in conjunction with other techniques if it is deemed necessary.

We now know that, for our subject, there is a *sub-conscious mathematical* grouping of HEIGHT, IN-FERIORITY, SEX, JEALOUSY and MARRIAGE. His *TD* symbol for this grouping is 3, representing basic insecurity, just as 3 itself is indicative of forces scattered, questions asked, general flurries of confusion.

GIRL, for our subject, totals 9, the symbol (check *What The Numbers Symbolize)* of completion. *No other word carries this total for our subject.* His sub-conscious here provides us with one of his basic goals, as indicated by his initial total of 5. In attempting to achieve his goal, he has created a wall of obstacles based on a general feeling of inferiority and frustration, as indicated by the 3 total groupings.

His 5 subconscious indicator tells us, initially, what he needs, desires, attempts, wants—but this goal (conceivably, even very likely—marriage)—is obscured by the fact that marriage is colored (for him) with CONFUSION (3), and this confusion applies to his other 3 groupings, that is, not only marriage itself, but sex, inferiority in connection with height and jealousy.

What we want to know is what does represent self-confidence for our subject—and he gives us a psychological clue through his *TD* total of 5 for SELF-CONFIDENCE, which is the same as his initial or subconscious thoughts total. This number (5), we already know, has to do with sex, just as the number 8 does.

What do we find when we look for 5 or 8 totals? Under 5, we have his general subconscious total, and we also have AMERICA and SELF-CONFIDENCE. We now know that our subject associates being in AMERICA with SELF-CONFIDENCE.

The need for love is evident and LOVE, for our subject, presents a problem similar to marriage, in that his total is 7, showing another kind of confusion—self-deception. Other 7 totals include SAFETY and WORK.

Our subject is telling us, *through his subconscious,* that he will feel economically SAFE when he finds the "right" WORK and this will automatically result in the finding of LOVE. Love will bring him what he basically seeks (he tells us through his totals): a home. The classical *TD* symbol for home is 6. For our subject, MONEY is symbolized by that total. He is telling us a story so startlingly clear!

It should, at this time, be most definitely noted that the words given in this test are not arbitrary. Students and psychologists are urged to suggest other word lists, eliminating some, adding others, always varying to an extent—depending upon the subject or the patient and his problems as he states them, or as indicated through other techniques, either horoscopic or via orthodox procedures.

It is time, now, to have a look at the external Mr. X, although this "look" came about (factors revealed to the author by the subject's psychologist) *after* the *TD* findings were noted.

Age: 32. Born in Czechoslovakia. Taken to Germany and placed in concentration camp, May, 1944. Permitted to come to America in December, 1946. Feels he is "too short." Has inferiority about his "lack of height." Is concerned about the "right kind of girl" for himself. Concerned also about the "right job."

These external or "conscious" revelations were most clearly perceived through use of the *TD* technique.

Remember: this was not a post-mortem—our *TD* factors were given BEFORE Mr. X's case history was made known!

We never saw him, so had no idea about his HEIGHT, but through his number groupings *(TD* technique) he told us: INFERIORITY and HEIGHT (3), as well as SEX, JEALOUSY, MARRIAGE.

The psychologist treating Mr. X was able to provide immeasurable aid through this *TD* test. It is only the beginning of what the author positively believes will prove a boon, both to practitioner and patient.
Where we go from here—and how far—depends upon further experiment by *others,* by laymen and by qualified persons in a variety of fields.

The practitioner can help the patient to recognize what is buried in his subconscious, can provide corrective therapy once the patient is able to *mathematically recognize* some of his innermost conflicts.

We have provided one example, admittedly incomplete, for the potential goes beyond our present knowledge. There were other experiments with similarly encouraging results. Our *TD* technique, in this case, was able to reveal WHY Mr. X showed decided tendencies to withdraw, to indulge in self-doubt and pity, as well as abuse at the hands of others. He was lethargic and felt he wasn't "good enough."

Thought Dial helped us and him to understand the *why* of these feelings of insecurity and confusion with regard to his basic wants, needs, desires, wishes, hopes, dreams, ambitions.

I leave it to other students and experiments to determine further conclusions, such as the grouping of DOCTOR and MATURITY (8). We also have COUSIN and CHILDREN (4). MOTHER is 1. SISTER-IN-LAW provides the only double number, 11.

This *new dimension* can and should be used in conjunction with other sections of the *TD*.

And now we break down this technique to individual words, to provide further examples and help round out this aspect of *TD*.

For astrological students, Mr. X's birthdate: September 15, 1926, hour unknown. City and state, unknown. Country: Czechoslovakia.

FURTHER ASPECTS OF THE

NEW DIMENSION

As an individual's life changes, so do his opinions, prejudices, inclinations, desires—and *thoughts*. Some persons are basically mature when it comes to ideas concerning such abstracts as LOVE or SUCCESS, while others display marked infantile tendencies. Use of *Thought Dial* helps us and the subject to obtain clear insight to what might otherwise remain vague abstractions. This technique represents a further aspect of the new dimension of *TD*.

Let us take, as our first example, the word LOVE. The subject is told to think of LOVE—and to dial or instantaneously select three numbers, which are added in the usual way, until a single number between 1 and 9 is left, the only double numbers retained being 11 and 22. Incidentally, by "instantaneous," we do not necessarily mean "speedy." The time taken to select the numbers will vary with the individual. Some persons are able to dial the numbers quickly; others choose with what might be termed "deliberate speed."

Experiments conducted during the past six months tend to indicate that THE MORE MATURE THE IN-DIVIDUAL . . . the more likely he is to dial or select numbers which total 6 when it comes to the word LOVE.

133

The following is a general break-down and analysis of each of the *TD* totals in connection with LOVE. To repeat, the subject is told to think of the word LOVE, of what LOVE means to him, or what he wishes it could be—he concentrates on LOVE and then makes his number selection. The result provides us with a valuable key to our subject as far as his subconscious picture of LOVE is concerned.

LOVE

The interpretations that follow are based on recent tests; the core of the meanings are provided and are purposely presented in a relatively "light" vein. As in other sections of *TD*, it is up to the operator to add dimension as he gains skill and insight.

TOTALS:

ONE—For you, love is romance! It is a new world, a world almost detached from the one in which you are now living. Your subconscious reactions show that you are sincere, that you are looking for the "one person," and that when you find him—(or her) there will be plenty of love! What you must avoid is an attitude of selfishness, which exhibits itself occasionally and which would not be at all satisfactory in connection with love.

TWO—Love, or the thought of it, often depresses you! You are not fond of chasing or being chased. You prefer security and the sanity of a steady routine. Love, for you, represents maturity: a home of your own, a family, children upon whom you can shower your affection. Your attitude is stable, commendable. But, remember, in order to find love, you must seek it! Prince Charming (or Princess) is not likely to appear out of nowhere. Which means you must avoid getting into a rut in either your attitudes or actions.

THREE—Frivolous is the word for your attitude toward love! At least that's true for the present. Love, according to your projective psychology total, represents a gay social whirl. And you are not at all anxious to settle down! You prefer to look over the field. That's fine, perhaps even commendable at this time. But, later, as you grow older, more sure of yourself and what you are seeking in a life partner, this will change. You will become more selective. But for right now—have fun! Wholesome contacts with members of the opposite sex will help solidify your ideas of love.

FOUR—Love, for you, is friendship intensified! Which is not bad, not bad at all. It represents—this projective psychological total—a grown-up attitude toward emotional well-being. Your attitude is one of steadiness. You are not one to run hither and yon— rather, you prefer loyalty. You will find that you are most likely to be attracted to those who exhibit qualities of thrift, steadfastness and sincerity.

FIVE—For you, love means family: it means children and also physical and mental attractiveness. Your attitude is based on a combination of the family unit and romance with a capital "R!" You feel, according to this test, that you will travel in connection with love. Perhaps your thoughts are concentrated on education, college—for the test total shows that love means learning to you. Higher learning. Which, in a sense, is what love is!

SIX—Domesticity is your keyword in connection with love. Your subconscious attitude is one of home, family and a sweet, considerate mate. It would appear, from this total, that you possess qualities of maturity worthy of the wisest adult. On this, congratulations! Your love life should be rich and full. And it's a good bet you'll have a home picked out before taking any steps down the aisle! Your attitude, your thoughts concerning love are practical and reasonable.

SEVEN—Why do you have such a long face when

you think about love? It can be fun, you know! As a matter of fact, it should be. Finding the right person, sharing your life with one you love represents fulfillment of man's fondest wish. Your total, however, reveals that you have misgivings. On the positive side, this is fine; it makes you selective, discriminating. But, negatively, it could represent an attitude best described as "too fussy." Loosen up! Combine good taste, discrimination with an open mind—and heart.

EIGHT—Love and money make a wonderful combination—and this takes the words right out of your mouth! You think of love as the most important thing in your life. You are certainly as romantic, if not more so, than the next person. However, your projective number total reveals that you tie in money with a happy love life. There is nothing wrong in doing so! But emotional maturity dictates that you acquire a sense of proportion. Life consists of love, material possessions — and lots of other things, too. Think it over—carefully!

NINE—Your sense of "love" is universal! That is, you associate love with generosity, well-being, with world peace, with idealism put into practice. This is commendable! Your projective number total reveals that you could never be happy with a person who was cruel or selfish, or self-centered. Your own nature appears to be giving; your goals are altruistic. When you find love—you will be finding life!

ELEVEN—When it comes to love, your ideas are apt to be considered "unconventional." Love, for you, means reaching up to, and entering, a new realm. The *TD* total here is indicative of a person who regards love as almost fatalistic: there are occult or "destiny" implications—it is almost as if you are convinced the matter is out of your hands. There are two extremes here, one positive and the other negative. On the positive side, your attitude toward love is mature in that you are not seeking perfection. On the negative side, you are so "destiny-minded" about love, that you are completely passive: you wait and wait for your "love" to come riding up on a white charger.

TWENTY-TWO: Love means power here: the power of a life-providing force. You are idealistic, perhaps to a fault, in your attitude toward this emotion. Your job is to arrive at a "definition of terms" within yourself. There is no room for confusion, which means you cannot afford to delay a process of intensive self-analysis in connection with LOVE. Love, for you, is likely to mean beauty, but also problems involving PHYSICAL aspects of relations with members of the opposite sex. Greater happiness indicated when you overcome rigid or fixed attitudes.

MONEY

Let us experiment, at this time, with a new *operating* technique. We have already stated that the actual dial of *TD* is a mantram, a procedure, a method of "drawing out" numerical aspects of the subconscious. Now, for the following tests, we temporarily eliminate the dial. Understand, the dial *can* be used here, or *eliminated,* as the operator prefers.

Much of this material was prepared for the national magazine, *'TEEN'*, and the interpretations are aimed at younger individuals, persons in their 'teens.

I am reproducing this material *almost* as it appeared, in order to stimulate *desire for experiment* within readers. It is my point that processes of *TD* are limitless: what this eventually will come to mean to the future is a matter of *exciting conjecture.* How soon final conclusions are arrived at depend upon this type of variation and experiment.

Here we will read interpretations purposely aimed at young persons: but the kernel of general or over-all meaning is contained and will enable the student to add material and to verify past definitions.

Psychologists say humans are very much interested in three things—in the following order: LOVE, MONEY and HEALTH.

Through our instantaneous number selection technique, we have already examined YOUR reaction (what you *really* think) to love. Now, let's explore your subconscious attitude toward MONEY.

All of us, whether "poetic" or materialistic, are living in a civilization where money has assumed tremendous import. We are not saying this is right or wrong. But it exists—and insight to *your* subconscious attitude toward money may help you now, and also later, when you assume the responsibilities that accompany adulthood.

Our test is simple. Concentrate on the word MONEY. Then check or circle any of the three numbers in our table below:

$$1 \quad 2 \quad 3$$
$$4 \quad 5 \quad 6$$
$$7 \quad 8 \quad 9$$
$$11 \quad 22$$

Now, add your numbers from left to right until you arrive at a single total between 1 and 9. For example, suppose you select 4, 2 and 7. Adding, the total is 13. Now, adding 13, we arrive at 1 plus 3, or a final answer of 4. Retain only 11 and 22 as double numbers.

Use this psychological technique to test your own subconscious reaction to MONEY. Simply concentrate on the word—then select àny of the three numbers provided. Then add from left to right until you arrive at a single-digit total. When you do, check below for your inner thoughts concerning MONEY.

If your total is ONE: Money, in itself, is not particularly impressive as far as you are concerned. What *does* impress you is the *manner* in which money is obtained. You gain pleasure from finances only if the gaining of income comes about through inventiveness, originality, and pioneering action. You will gain most through your own creative efforts and by your ability to attract those who, in turn, seem able to attract money! Your subconscious reaction to money is, "I like it, but it by no means makes up for everything." In other words, you are the idealist who rates LOVE over money!

If your total is TWO: All in all, you are *passive* about money! It would indeed be difficult to "buy" you. It is a case, most definitely, of having to *win* you. You do not judge either yourself, or others, by the amount of cash on hand. Money, according to your subconscious reaction, represents SECURITY, especially in connection with the home, with family and children. But, as an end in itself, money is very likely to leave you cold! You can gain financial independence by being diplomatic—you lose out if you attempt to force issues. Your inner thoughts about money are serene. And this indeed is a nice, a very nice mental set-up!

If your total is THREE: Your subconscious reaction reveals that you are apt to associate MONEY with LUCK. And who can say—maybe you're right! However, this instantaneous number selection total indicates that you tend toward extravagance—often you may fail to realize the value of money. In some ways, this can be a charming characteristic. But, in other ways, it is not only *not* practical, but downright dangerous! Learn to consider the feelings of others—where money is concerned. Realize that some people take an attitude toward cash that is caused by genuine need. Thus, your sense of humor about financial matters could strike those persons as odd—or inconsiderate. Where your own pocketbook is concerned—it will probably keep you well satisfied. Congratulations!

If your total is FOUR: Your attitude toward money is apt to be quite serious. Constructively, this is fine: it shows you know the value of money and are willing to work in order to obtain financial security. However, on the negative side, there is a tendency for you to become gloomy and moody—to brood over whether you have "enough." The latter should be avoided. Remember, what counts is doing your best — the rewards (financial and otherwise) will follow. Being morose does not help. It is good to be economical and practical. But it is not so good if you become a "tightwad." In all, success is shown—but you have to work for what you get. No one, it seems, is going to be giving things away, at least not to you.

If your total is FIVE: Your selection-total reveals that, very often, you associate money with TRAVEL. And with romance! Money, at its best, represents (to you) change, travel, variety, affairs of the heart. This may be a misconception: others will tell you that your attitude will change as you grow older. They may be right—these well-meaning persons—where they themselves are concerned! But your thoughts, your attitude, your feelings are right for you! Now, how to go about becoming financially secure? Well, your number total would indicate that you gain through communications, through writing, self-expression, acting, and other creative endeavors—or through the "agenting" or selling of creative efforts. Book publishing, authors' agent, syndicate-feature selling—these might all appeal to you. Anyway, the odds are that you will have money—and romance!

If your total is SIX: Money, to you, often means HARMONY .In other words, you associate an abundance of cash with the erasure of worry or friction. Who is to say you are wrong? Subconsciously, money is a necessity to you where marriage, where travel or almost any adventure is concerned. You are not a fanatic about money—but you have a sure, practical, mature, adult view toward that commodity. There is nothing sensational or "funny" in your attitude. It is based on a realistic, sound approach. It is also interesting to note that you associate money with family—with the ability to help loved ones. This is commendable—as is your entire attitude—revealed by the numbers you selected and their individual total.

If your total is SEVEN: You are not at all sure of yourself when it comes to money. There is a tendency, revealed here, for you to regard money in a rather mysterious light. Where does it come from? Where does it go? Those are questions you often ask yourself, according to your subconscious number indicator. You should try to be more down-to-earth where finances are concerned. Make an effort toward budgeting yourself— you seem prone to make mistakes along these lines. You deceive yourself into thinking you have too much —or too little. Money usually comes to you from unexpected sources, and at unexpected times—at least so it would seem from this total. Would you think it too distasteful to bone up on accounting, or economics? It would certainly be to your advantage to do so!

If your total is EIGHT: Money appears to be second nature to you! You associate money with power—and with members of the opposite sex. Your subconscious reaction to "money" is active indeed! There is no half-way where you and money are concerned. It is either all the way—or nothing at all. Your obvious lesson is one of BALANCE—the obtaining of a sense of balance. Otherwise, you tend to have PLENTY OF NOTHING. Do not make the mistake of judging people by the size of their bank accounts. Money doesn't make a person either "good" or "bad." At all times, it is the individual who counts—not how much or how little cash he has on deposit. In all, you appear assured of money—if intense interest in a subject has anything at all to do with acquisition.

If your total is NINE: For you, money seems to represent UNIVERSAL APPEAL. Your attitude is that "money makes the world go 'round." You may be right, too! But it takes more than money alone to make things happen: your subconscious number selection reveals that indeed you are very aware of this fact. However, money is also a matter of PRIDE to you. Having enough cash enables you to fulfill wishes, to help others, to "get around." As far as you are concerned—money is required in order to fully express your potential. Your sights are set high—your goal is universal. Your "costs" are secondary to your objective. With this kind of an attitude, money is really secondary. The indications are that you will succeed!

If your total is ELEVEN: You are likely to be most concerned with *how* you make your money. Money, in itself, might be secondary in importance. You tend (through your instantaneous number selection) to place more emphasis on the romantic, on devising sensational or unusual methods of acquiring capital. Money, for you, enhances you to *others*. This is significant. You, yourself, are not likely to feel any different, rich or poor. But you *project;* you wonder, for example, how Jill and Jim will feel once you have made your fortune. Or, on the opposite track, what they will think of you if you *fail* to become affluent. Recognize this tendency; deal with it, know it, master it. Live your own life, fulfill your *own* desires in money matters—be *less* concerned with what Jill or Jim will think. Basically, you are more likely to be happy through utilization of the occult or unusual or through progressive techniques in making your way in the material world.

If your total is TWENTY-TWO: Your subconscious

144

attitude toward money is one which could lead you to success in the world of commerce. You are not afraid. This is the significant point: not afraid to tear down in order to rebuild, not afraid to admit an error in order to start over on the right path. Money does not awe you. You have a healthy respect for it, but you are the MASTER and money is the MEDIUM, which is a constructive subconscious reaction. You hurt yourself when you *limit ideas*. Allow yourself to be EXPANSIVE. Do not be concerned about expense. Needling, or endless bickering can ruin chances for your success in money matters. Be practical as a BASIS FOR BUILDING. Be willing to TAKE LEAVE OF PRACTICALITY, as generally interpreted or understood by the majority, IN ORDER TO MAKE DREAMS TURN TO RE-ALITIES.

SUCCESS

Success! It seems to be an American word, a peculiar American phenomenon — the drive for success, the striving for it, the thinking of it—the dream about it. Your dreams of success—the subconscious ones—often are buried deep, hidden from the conscious mind. But through our spontaneous number selection technique, often we are able to probe deep, shaking hands with the truth that inhabits us all.

Let us try our method on YOU and your subconscious thoughts regarding SUCCESS.

Success, of course, is many things to many persons. And as each of us reaches maturity, success or the lack of it assumes added importance. What you *think* about success may well have much to do with whether or not you are able to attain it. And your ideas, or thoughts, about that elusive commodity are probably entirely different from the notions held by the next person.

First, relax. Then, think of SUCCESS. When you have that word, or thought, clearly formed in your mind, check any three of the numbers shown below:

$$1 \quad 2 \quad 3$$
$$4 \quad 5 \quad 6$$
$$7 \quad 8 \quad 9$$
$$11 \quad 22$$

Now, add your three numbers and reduce to a single total between 1 and 9. Simply add from left to right until you arrive at a single number. Retain only 11 or 22 as double totals.

For example, suppose you checked the numbers 1, 5 and 6. Your total, of course, would be 12 (1 plus 5 plus 6). Then you add the 12 total from left to right until arriving at a single digit, which would be 3 (1 plus 2). A very simple procedure, but most revealing, as you will see when you read what your number total indicates about you—and SUCCESS!

IF YOUR TOTAL IS 1: Success, as far as you are concerned, means the blazing of new trails: it is being a pioneer, being independent, being able to make up your own mind and arrive at your own decisions. Your idea of success parallels some of the finest instincts of the founding fathers of this country. If you can live up to your subconscious concept of success—then there is little doubt you *will* be successful. Good luck!

IF YOUR TOTAL IS 2: Some of the guys and gals might think your notions of success denote laziness. But this is not necessarily so! It's just that you are fond of relaxation; you feel that success means the right to go fishing, or listen to the hi-fi set, or to do whatever your pleasure instincts dictate. Of course, carried to extreme, this subconscious notion could result in apathy. However, on the constructive side, your ideas about success could lead you into cultural fields, including the creative aspects of music and literature. Stick to your guns!

IF YOUR TOTAL IS 3: Your spontaneous number selection reveals an attitude toward success best described as "too much!" Key words are expansion, fortune and beauty, as well as luxury and money. In other words, you have an almost classic attitude toward success. In order to fulfill your dreams, however, you will have to avoid scattering your forces. You will have to finish what you start instead of riding off in all directions at once.

IF YOUR TOTAL IS 4: Success, to you, means hard work. Perhaps you have the most practical of all attitudes: you know there are obstacles to overcome and you appear quite willing to work your way up the ladder. Congratulations on a very realistic point of view! What you must make an effort to avoid is a tendency toward gloominess. Realize that success usually is built upon hard work. But don't lose your sense of humor when considering dream fulfillment. You can go very far indeed. Especially if you keep smiling!

IF YOUR TOTAL IS 5: For you, success is associated with travel, excitement, creative activity—and romance! Yes, your friends are right when they sometimes refer to you as an "incurable romantic!" When you think of success, according to your spontaneous number selection, you are thinking of recognition on an international scale. There is nothing halfway about your ideas: it is either all the way or nothing at all! Be willing to communicate ideas. To be able to do so means study, reading, appreciation of the arts and knowledge of current events. You may become one of our great detectives or journalists.

IF YOUR TOAL IS 6: Success, to you, has much to do with a happy home life, with marriage and children and domestic tranquility. In expressing this spontaneous number total, you reveal a mature attitude, and also you lessen the odds toward your goal. What you desire is not the spectacular, but a steady stream of happiness and warmth based on love. Many of your friends tell you not to be so sentimental: pay them no heed! A home of your own will play an increasingly important role in your life as you grow older. Success seems assured!

IF YOUR TOTAL IS 7: You are most idealistic in your concept of success. Your dreams are of perfection, of complete inner and outer harmony. Your thoughts are concerned with marriage, with the perfect or "dream" partner. This, of course, is not always easy to attain. But with this subconscious desire so strongly implanted—your chances are good! It is often difficult for you to define what you actually mean by "success." But you are not the type of person to compromise. The person you choose as your life partner—the one who will eventually share your dreams, hopes and wishes—will indeed be a lucky individual!

IF YOUR TOTAL IS 8: No beating around the bush with you! Success is money—you think of success as the power, the ability to achieve your heart's desire. Often, this is tied up with the material things of life. But, as you grow older and your best qualities develop, your ideas may well undergo gradual changes. Money is important. No one would deny that; but so are ideals and so is self-satisfaction that comes with a job well done. You will have a better chance of achieving your startlingly high goals once materialism is suffused with a little of the light of altruism! In all, you are to be admired for dreaming so high up in the air!

IF YOUR TOTAL IS 9: Your idea of success is apt to be international publicity and acclaim. Your ideas are big ones! There is nothing petty about your thinking—conscious or subconscious. With you, it is all the way—to the top! You can best achieve success through the creative arts or by cultivating a sense of *appreciation* for the efforts of others. You are an idealist: you are sympathetic, you are the natural humanitarian. It would be wise to bet on your chances

—you are inclined TOWARD success!

IF YOUR TOTAL IS 11: Your subconscious re-action to SUCCESS is marked by a *deviation from the norm*. You envision yourself choosing by-ways that others fear or are not aware of—you are a pioneer when it comes to succeeding because your methods are "different." Once you begin to follow the worn and weary paths, you begin to wane. This subconscious indicator does warn, however, against being different just for the sake of sensationalism or of attracting attention. You could become a lonely, unhappy person unless you are *thoroughly schooled* in your field of endeavor, which might well be television, aviation, astrology, ESP or work with techniques outlined here. Follow first impressions; your intuition should be of tremendous aid to you.

IF YOUR TOTAL IS 22: For a young person, your basic success attitudes are marked by mature development. Deep within, you tend to associate success with personal magnetism, with persuasiveness—with a winning personality. You recognize values of SALESMANSHIP. This will stand you in good stead, UNLESS YOU SWING TOWARD OUT-AND-OUT COMMERCIALISM. Your attitudes (subconscious indicator) are unique and attractive only in that they promote a FASCINATING UNIQUENESS of approach. Avoid the "heavy hand." Tell your story, sell yourself with a SUBTLE touch. Otherwise, you will be laughed at instead of listened to—and remember that nothing is likely to be permanent except CHANGE (which means be willing to retrace your steps or original ideas in order to arrive at your greatest potential).

WHOM YOU ATTRACT

This test attempts to tell you something about the man or woman you attract. And the results should also give you some pertinent information about yourself as well as persons who are attracted to you.

Simply relax and think of or visualize your ideal man or woman, as the case may be. Then check any three numbers below:

1	3	5	7	11	22
2	4	6	8	9	

Add the total of your number selections and reduce to a single digit between 1 and 9. The only double numbers retained as final totals are 11 and 22.

TOTALS:

ONE—Those members of the opposite sex, attracted to you, are NOT apt to be shrinking violets. Instead, they tend to be forceful, dominant, original, independent. They may aspire to the theatre, the world of entertainment. Those attracted to you have sex appeal, are able to project their personalities—and may very well be temperamental to an extreme!

TWO—You seem to attract true romantics! Mostly, they are steadfast, loyal, and have an eye to the future —as well as stars in their eyes. You are warned, however, that frivolous action—on your part—could disillusion them and finally drive them away. You tend to attract those who have an appreciation of home life and home cooking! You attract (and are attracted to) persons who have their eyes pointed toward the heavens and their feet firmly on the ground.

THREE—Members of the opposite sex who are intrigued by you are very likely to be those who love parties, who are happiest when the subject matter is light, and who have boundless energy. You may, at times, have trouble keeping up with your admirers! They are apt to be considered "lucky" in that they generally appear HAPPY. Those who are drawn to you are persons who like to travel, who have respect for education, but who "skip over" their studies and thus attain only superficial knowledge. Others may tend to be jealous of your good fortune in attracting such gay individuals. Be wary, however, or you may find yourself completely scattering your forces.

FOUR—Those of the opposite sex, attracted to you, are apt to be solid, steady and strong. These fellows (or girls) are great admirers of the truth. You get along with them by being forthright, honest, by speaking from the heart. If anyone can tag a phoney, the people you attract certainly can! You are lucky. Those attracted to you are not out to fool you.

FIVE—You attract persons who abound in sex appeal! Yes, those who really dig you are filled with life, creative forces, are apt to be artists, writers, entertainers, or follow a line of endeavor which emphasizes self-expression. You must be quite a person yourself to attract these members of the opposite sex! To have continued social success, keep up with the world. Read and pursue a creative hobby. Otherwise, you will be by-passed!

SIX—Those of the opposite sex—drawn to you—are lovers of luxury, the finer things of life, including good music and books. You attract what might be termed people with a sense of maturity. No child-play here. Which means you have a challenge on your hands! You, too, must be grown-up, must have adult tastes. You are to be complimented. Those you attract appear to have a great sense of discrimination!

SEVEN—Members of the opposite sex, interested in you, are apt to be moody, independent to the 'nth degree, and very serious indeed! It is up to you, very often, to inject some humor into the situation. You attract fellows (or girls) who are concerned with abstract principles. They know the meanings of words like *integrity* and *honesty* and *sincerity*. And they are usually quoting poetry!

EIGHT—Fellows (or girls) attracted to you are the business leaders of the future! They talk and act big—and can usually back it up! Seriously, these people have a sense of responsibility. They are not afraid of hard work. They like money but are not fanatical on the subject. But just don't try to borrow without offering collateral! You are to be congratulated—you attract members of the opposite sex who will be sought after in the future.

NINE—You interest members of the opposite sex who truly are idealists! So, you must be quite an individual in your own right. The people who lean toward you are fiery in their beliefs. They will not compromise on principles. They are very sympathetic and always side with the underdog. One of them could turn out to be world famous! To keep up with the people you attract—you must make yourself familiar with art, music and literature.

ELEVEN—You fascinate persons whose interests border on the unusual: astrology, graphology, palmistry, numerology, modern art, underground elements in modern literature, etc. The man or woman drawn to you (and by the same token—the *kind* of man or woman you *desire* to attract) is a SEARCHER, a SEEKER, one who is never satisfied with the status quo—one who believes in TRUTH as AUTHORITY—one who feels truth is not always to be found in textbooks. These men or women are certainly out-of-the-ordinary and they will instruct you and entertain you. Never turn away when they need help. If you neglect friends, you are going against your basic desires.

TWENTY-TWO—Your subconscious indicator here points to attraction of men or women who are creative, idealistic, who can teach the world many vital truths. Because you attract this type of individual, you are basically an exciting, challenging person, one who may eventually be associated with the communications media: publishing, radio, television, etc. Your key word is CREATE. Once you become smug or eternally satisfied with things as they are, you are on the road toward loss of friends—and loss of a vital part of yourself.

SOUNDS AND WORDS

We have now examined a NEW DIMENSION of *TD* and have also looked into further aspects of that dimension. Once again, I would like to stress the importance of experiment: with word lists, individual words, ideas, etc., including new or different techniques and applications.

Numbers can take us to the source, to the very beginnings of thought, perhaps of life. Nature is geometric, is geometrized: if we but look and *absorb* the possibilities are limitless.

Personally, I would be most interested in hearing of experiments with *TD* in connection with SOUND. I am of the opinion that letters, the consonants and the vowels can, in some manner, be discerned through *TD* techniques. Where did the alphabet come from, where did it originate? Dr. Hugh A. Moran, in his masterful work, *The Alphabet and the Ancient Calendar**, tells us of ASTROLOGICAL ELEMENTS IN THE ORIGIN OF THE ALPHABET. He puts forth the idea that the *letters of the phonetic alphabet are based on the signs of the Luna Zodiac,* which long preceded the twelve zodiacal signs of the ecliptic or Solar Zodiac. Although the Luna Signs are older than the Solar, the latter goes back at least to the 4th millennium B.C. As Dr. Moran points out, by the time anyone began to wonder WHERE the alphabet letters came from, the source was obscured or lost to the Western world.

*Pacific Books, Palo Alto, Calif. (1953)

However, astrology, as admitted by Dr. Moran, has "left as a heritage for mankind their greatest tool of learning, and one of the most important assets of civilization—the phonetic alphabet." The letters of the alphabet, it turns out, may well (are very likely, according to Dr. Moran and other scholars) be associated with astrological signs. In turn, each *letter* is related to a numerical symbol. Somewhere, in-between, may be the key, the answer, the clue to a line of experimenting which, perhaps in the not-too-distant-future, will enable us to discern *names* and *words* as well as abstract thoughts through use of *TD*.

Dr. Moran states that, "Symbols derived from the heavens form parts of the personal pronouns, the verb 'to be,' the ideas of birth, life and death, the blooming of flowers and the numerical system." The language, without these symbols, would be dead, while with them, "it is capable of expressing the most abstruse philosophy."

Let us hope we will be in a position to delve deeper into this aspect of *Thought Dial* when the time for the third edition rolls around.

—Sydney Omarr
Los Angeles, Calif.
December, 1958

BOOK REVIEWS

THOUGHT DIAL
by Sydney Omarr

Scientific interest in the "unconscious" has been a major development in the twentieth century. Among those exploring it and who are still living, no one is more distinguished than Carl Jung, world renowned psycho-therapist. As Sydney Omarr states in this fascinating new book, Jung's work had an important influence on him in the development of this new technique for tapping the unconscious. Mr. Omarr, well-known as an astrologer in the United States, has for many years been interested also in numerology. THOUGHT DIAL is an attempt to combine numerology, astrology and depth psychology. On the basis of tests of its actual effectiveness one must record a marked success.

On one occasion my wife and I consulted the THOUGHT DIAL to find a lost mailing list; we had turned our apartment upside down to find it without any success and spent a half day in fruitless search. According to the THOUGHT DIAL, the lost object would be found in the southeast corner of the main room. But, in addition,

it indicated that the object was in something and that it had been put there in anger and haste. This was exactly so in every respect and thus we found it. A friend of ours, who is a fine psychiatrist, has been testing THOUGHT DIAL for months and has been very much impressed with it. Comments on the book by a number of well-known people. including the writers, Henry Miller and Tiffany Thayer, have been very favorable. too. The book is written intelligently by Mr. Omarr, especially in his endeavors to explain WHY the THOUGHT DIAL should be able to give significant answers to questions asked.

THOUGHT DIAL has already gone into an enlarged, second edition and is prefaced by a valuable introduction by Carl Payne Tobey, one of our most brilliant contemporary astrological researchers and teachers. Whether the reader uses it for entertainment or more seriously for psychological probing, a copy of THOUGHT DIAL is worth having.

(*Editor's Note: This review first appeared in the Winter, 1959. issue of IN SEARCH, an international astrological quarterly, edited by Charles A. Jayne, Jr.*)

THOUGHT DIAL
by SYDNEY OMARR

This remarkable, probably unique book presents a mechanical device, and a mantic (Greek *mantikos*, "prophetic") procedure for "tapping the unconscious," which seems to belong to the same family as Edison's projected "Telephone between Worlds," the tumbler, planchette, Ouija Board, pendulum, as well as psychometry, telepathy, hypnotism, psychic faculties in general, numerology, and astrology.

With the book comes a card with clock-face and pointer, the circle numbered 0 to 9, also 11 and 22. The technique is to relax, form a clear thought or question, place a finger on the pointer, and induce or instruct your subconscious to dial three numbers; add the digits of these, let us say 8, 5, 2, making 15; add the 1 and 5, to make 6: that is your answer. If, however, the total comes to 11 or 22, do not add the digits but take the numbers as they are.

About half the book is taken up with describing the significance of the numbers and their connection with Subconscious Thoughts: Direct Questions: Locating lost articles: Picking Winners: Sound and Color: Parts of the Body: Love: Money: Success.

Fundamental is the thesis that every item in the universe is associated with, represented by, a number, not by man's thinking, but intrinsically. As Pythagoras said: "Nature ever geometrizes." "Number is an archetype of order, which has become conscious" (Jung). Numbers are "objects in themselves . . . abstractions representing symbols of thoughts or ideas." Hence the Thought Dial, an "instrument for measuring and analyzing intangibles such as thoughts, questions, speculations, is basically YOU."

Another thesis, held by Jung and accepted as a working theory by Omarr, is that all knowledge comes from or through the subconscious, which is the seat of memory, the memory of an individual being "probably indestructible, written in indelible script in space and time . . . an eternal part of a Cosmos in development," a dictum from Dr. Stromberg, who (as do many others) thinks that the brain receives waves from the "universal brain," the "soul of the universe."

Whatever you may think of the theory, Omarr presents substantial evidence that, empirically—often even with beginners—it works. There seems, in fact, no department of life beyond the range of this numerical technique.

The establishment of such a "telephone" between the subconscious and the conscious is so intriguing, apparently so full of promise, simple and practical, that the urge to experiment is almost irresistible.

I recommend the book and suggest that readers who obtain it report results. The basic plan—which, of course, may well be modified by experience—may prove to be a landmark in psychic research, and of immense value in practical life.— *Arthur E. Powell.*

THIRD EDITION

THOUGHT DIAL and its history becomes more and more intriguing: the time for the third edition *has* rolled around. The work has become a minor classic in the sense that it not only appeals to those intrigued with new thought or Uranian subjects, but because it has attracted the attention of those who ordinarily are inclined to scoff in this area. I do not want to dwell on this — it is discouraging. Only "off the record" are most of the "surprising" advocates willing to talk or write. This, in itself, is a psychological phenomenon. Perhaps the reasons why THOUGHT DIAL remains "underground" are founded in our economic system: a leading scientist at a leading university does not want to risk his position by openly discussing the work. A philosopher and author wants it known that TD has provided much help for himself and his family — wants it known to the author, but *not to the public*. Doctors and psychiatrists use TD to personal and professional advantage, but this information — they make clear— is *off the record*. All right. So be it. Maybe by the time it is time for the fourth or fifth, or sixth edition, times will change. Perhaps. So TD is a "classic" in this sense. It is also a publishing phenomenon because of its price. It is a small book in the physical sense, but the price is admittedly a big one. Yet, it has become a best-seller in its field: the third edition is here and it is not unlikely it will run into ten or more editions. Part of the story of TD is the reaction to it *on the record*. Rather than quote numerous letters and comments, let us here reproduce two reviews, both dated August, 1959 — one in *Fate Magazine*, the other in *Search:*

Between the time of the second edition and this, the third, I have been contracted by the *New York Herald Tribune Syndicate* to write a five-day-a-week column on TD. The column, for reasons best known to the Syndicate, is called, THINK-A-DIGIT. In it, the reader thinks of a question—chooses three numbers and reduces them to a single digit—and is enabled to find the answer to his question in the column. As is surely obvious, the principle is the principle of TD. The more circulation, the more "exposure" this technique receives, the closer we come to the truth, to added information—to ultimate wisdom. It is for this reason that I take the space here to urge you to ask your local newspaper editor about THINK-A-DIGIT, to inform him it is available through the *New York Herald Tribune Syndicate.*

* * *

As you will note in the *second* edition (*Sounds the Words*), I had expressed the hope that we would be able actually to discern sounds—perhaps names — through use of TD. This, so far, has not come to pass. I still feel this is a distinct possibility. I urge further research.

* * *

I have been surprised to note that great success has been reported in sections dealing with selecting winners and locating lost objects. These were admittedly "theoretical" sections in

159

that actual experiments were limited. The answering of direct questions and subconscious thoughts were sections based on 10 or more years of research. The success there was more or less expected: we had proven it to ourselves. But now there are reports of astounding results in the "theoretical areas" and because of this we cannot but be encouraged in our hope that one day TD can be applied to *sound,* to the discerning of *letters,* or *initials* or actual *names.*

* * *

In the second edition *(Up To Now),* mention was made of the writing of Dr. Wilhelm Stekel, of Vienna, a psychiatrist who appeared familiar with the use of numbers in his work. He was brought to our attention by San Francisco photographer Harry Redl. We had asked for more information. Fortunately, we found our information in the form of Dr. Stekel's, *The Meaning and Psychology of Dreams.** This is a valuable work and has been translated and reprinted in pocketbook format. Stekel it termed "one of Freud's most distinguished collaborators." What he states about symbols in general, and numbers specifically, is rewarding, especially to the student of TD.

Our independent research, combined with the new treasurefind of Stekel, should ultimately result in *Thought Dial and Your Dreams.* Work is now underway on this project. As always, we would like to hear from you with regard to suggestions, ideas, experiences—particularly in relation to dreams and numbers, dreams interpreted via use of TD principles.

—Sydney Omarr
Los Angeles, Calif.
September, 1959

*Bard Books, Avon Publications, New York

PUBLISHER'S NOTE

Readers interested in keeping up with *Thought Dial* news, developments and experiments, are invited to request free copies of *Open Letter,* which is edited by Sydney Omarr.

Ninth House Publishing Co.
Box 1092
Hollywood 28, California

Perhaps sooner than expected, it is time for the fourth edition of THOUGHT DIAL.

The addition to the work shall, at this time, consist of a reproduction of a letter from Ariel Yvon Taylor. It was through her special course and her book, *Numerology Made Plain*, that I gained my first real knowledge — so many years ago — of the wonderful world of numbers. I had never had any personal contact with Miss Taylor, nor had we had any correspondence. But one day I did send her a copy of THOUGHT DIAL. Her letter, which follows, makes me, once again, know there is a purpose in our efforts — and that this book, this work will continue for many more editions and, it is hoped, eventually be filled with additional, absorbing truth.

In the meantime, I have completed another work, HENRY MILLER: HIS WORLD OF URANIA. In that book, now available from the present publisher, the language of astrology, in connection with the outpouring of a great American writer, is examined and analyzed. I believe it to be an excellent companion piece to THOUGHT DIAL.

Now, let us hear from Ariel Yvon Taylor — her letter dated May 31, 1960:

The only reason you have not heard from us with an earlier deep THANK YOU for your marvelous THOUGHT DIAL is that this is the first day since it came that we have had time to read it through, discover your kindly and charitable mention of the writer, and

bring an answer to a very important query, through the simple technique and Inspirational Answer which you bring.

The students we have would all like a copy.

No doubt you have my NUMEROLOGY — its FACTS and SECRETS, put out by C. & R. Anthony — 'Master Publications," or I would gladly send you a copy. They made a reprint of the major part of an earlier book, "Character-Grams" and added much new material on the birth date, showing our inclusion of the number of the Astrological Sign in the full date of birth. This we find is essential.

Our chapter on "Charomancy" was a brief Question and Answer game, based on interpretation of Four numbers. But it cannot hold a candle to your THOUGHT DIAL, which is the "Last Word" in making the Abstract, Concrete. Your highly intuitive faculty has given such wonderfully exact answers to every question one might ask, that every one really is taken back with amazement.

The big question around here for months has been, "Can we remain in Carnegie Hall, or will we have to move?" The THOUGHT DIAL said, "WAIT and SEE — No News, Good News." And so it has been. While half the building is now empty, we are still here, and plan to stay, with expectation of new management coming in any day from now on.

We are so grateful to Providence that some one with your high intelligence and splendid standing, has brought forth such a lucid, clear presentation of the practical use of Numbers, coupled with its high purpose in tapping the Universal Source of all Good.

You have given Numbers a king-sized robe to wear, and have brought forth a challenge to every Pythagorean of the present day to bring forth still greater fruit through greater research, in this secret key to the Unknown, which everyone seeks.

Just now I asked the THOUGHT DIAL for an answer as to where to focus our attention in the immediate future and it was surprising how exact it was — in the direction of which we had been thinking — "writing, syndicate feature-selling."

You have made clear more than any writer of the present day, that "Number, like Music, speaks a universal language." As John Ruskin said,

> "All life is music,
> When you touch the note right
> And in tune."

Here's to the Harmony of the Spheres, in that human understanding which you have made possible. Ever more Light and Power to YOU!

Gratefully ever,
ARIEL YVON TAYLOR

FIFTH EDITION

Once more, a new edition: it is hoped that the popularity of THOUGHT DIAL coincides with proof that its principles, properly applied, produce results. From communications received, this does appear to be the case. It is important that we hear from you regarding the outcome of your experiments; many of these communications will appear in the next or Sixth Edition, as well as being reported in OPEN LETTER.

Incidentally, note the communication from Ariel Yvon Taylor in the Fourth Edition: THOUGHT DIAL proved correct. That master of numbers *remains* in her office at Carnegie Hall!

The most surprising result of research, both personal and based on reports from around the nation, is the validity of the section on "Locating Lost Articles." This was, along with the "Picking Winners" technique, admittedly speculative, when compared to the answering of direct questions and the tapping of the subconscious. Yet, startling results have been obtained.

It cannot be too often stressed that a *familiarity with the numbers* is essential. The printed word, after all, is static. It is there and it remains the same. But the *human, creative process* can be brought into play once the basics are absorbed: it is this process which results in the most effective, accurate interpretation of the symbols (numbers).

Ideally, one should not have to carry TD around in order to make use of its principles and technique. There should be *familiarity* enough so that a subject asking a question, and coming up with a total of 7, would bring an immediate response from the operator. There should be enough familiarity with 7 to enable the operator to inform the subject that this is a sensitive area, an area where self-deception is likely to enter. The subject, in bringing forth a total of 7, clearly indicates he is not really sure, is building something in his own mind, is creating a false enthusiasm . . . and, thus, should exercise caution, should be willing to wait or

164

to insist on at least a temporary delay. This would apply in business as well as personal matters.

In other words, the symbol which 7 represents should begin unfolding for the operator, just as the number 1 would: independence, greater self-confidence, a step in a new direction, often involving dealings with the public, or communicating to large numbers of persons. While 7 would advocate delay — number 1 would push forward. Because 1 is related to the Sun, which, in its turn relates to Leo (the natural Fifth Zodiacal Sign), the subject giving this total in *thinking* of a question, often is concerned with some phase of "show business" or catering to the public: and, many times, his actions are sparked by a member of the opposite sex.

Familiarity! Become familiar with the numbers, so much so that a subject giving a series that totals 3 immediately tells you of confusion, a tendency to want to move too quickly, so quickly that the structure, the basis for that movement is, perhaps, not yet completed. Because 3 is associated with Jupiter (Sagittarius-Ninth House), these questions often are connected with "far-away" thoughts, perhaps literal long journeys . . . and much of the time with too much dependence on "luck."

So it should be with *all the numbers.* And all of these symbols, it should be remembered, are *many-sided.* Number 8 *is* money, but with money comes responsibility, authority, work, pressure. Demands are made (Saturn-Capricorn-Tenth House) by the community, by a member of the opposite sex (marriage); number 8, thus, brings a chance to "get ahead," but the subject must also be prepared for additional responsibility.

Please do use the technique explained in the chapter, "A New Dimension." Suppose, for example, a subject comes up with a 7 total. We know there is a disturbance (Neptune-Twelfth House) based on secret or inward fears: something the subject may not be admitting even to himself. Present a list of words: LOVER, HUSBAND (OR WIFE), CHILDREN, MONEY, CONTRACT, etc. Let the subject give numbers for those words, until (through techniques described in "A New Dimension") greater keys to the problem are obtained.

Above all, experiment until you are as familiar with the symbols represented by the numbers as you are by symbols relating to your own personal or special interests.

Use the principles of TD *daily* in your own life. Ask "Yes and No" questions; you will receive guidance, in this manner, on your own problems. You will know when to slow down (7) and when to speed up (1). And you will, through variations, gain greater insight to your own thinking, your attitudes toward different persons and situations in the areas encompassing everyday experiences.

— Sydney Omarr
Los Angeles
February, 1961

SIXTH EDITION

Completing a cycle, this new, sixth edition of THOUGHT DIAL is being issued by Llewellyn Publications, now located in St. Paul, Minnesota, under the direction of one of the most vital, new faces on the map of astrology and allied subjects. Carl L. Weschcke is the man. And he is going to take his place in the history of this field, as having had a most important part in bringing about its renaissance.

There have been new developments since the previous, fifth edition. One of the most important is the fact that I now am writing a daily, astrological column, syndicated around the world by General Features Corporation, of New York. If your favorite newspaper does not carry the column, this writer would be deeply indebted if you would write a note to your editor, or call him, asking him to contact General Features, in New York, about the Sydney Omarr astrology column.

I point up these facts, which perhaps have no *direct* connection with TD, because they reveal that work in this field is attracting greater interest. Other proofs: A recent issue of TIME Magazine referred to us as one of the "highbrows" in the field, a serious worker. And there have been numerous radio-television debates with astronomers and psychologists. And, each time, we get closer to the fact that astrology, and the principles of TD, are being more and more *accepted,* not rejected.

Of course the greatest example is the Tome you now are reading: The sixth edition of a book which is by no means an "easy" financial purchase. THOUGHT DIAL works. And *because* it works there has been a remarkable word-of-mouth campaign, which is more valuable than any formal advertising. That campaign has resulted in the selling-out of five editions. And now comes the sixth, being issued by Carl L. Weschcke, whose Llewellyn list of publications contains many "musts." *

* 100 S. Wabasha St
St Paul 7 Minnesota

I would like to dedicate this latest edition of TD to the many, many persons who have taken the trouble to write to me about their experiments, and their successes. There have been some reports of failure, too. But that number has been so small, that the success "stories" far out-number them. As a matter of fact, all of us interested in this work welcome reports, favorable or unfavorable. Only then can we arrive at the truth, which is our goal. But, as I say, the success reports win by an overwhelming majority. Perhaps this means that only those with remarkable results bother to report. Perhaps.

In today's mail, for example, a brief note from Wm. G. Bailey, of Delaware Park Manor, in Wilmington, Delaware: "I am having rather good luck with my book, THOUGHT DIAL, and would like a few copies of OPEN LETTER, edited by Sydney Omarr."

OPEN LETTER is a report issued at *irregular* periods, telling of books of interest in this field, and reporting on THOUGHT DIAL experiments.

Another note in the mail today comes from Willi Bentley, of Buffalo, New York: "I have your book, THOUGHT DIAL. It is wonderful. I use it all the time. And the answers come out right eight to nine times out of ten."

There are others. One day, perhaps, we will publish an auxiliary booklet, containing reports of experiments with THOUGHT DIAL, sent in by various readers. And I also look forward to the day when we can, with the aid of ac-credited psychologists, conduct *disciplined* experiments designed to tell us how far — or the opposite — we can go with the dynamic principles uncovered in the use of TD. Those days are not far away!

Here is another communication, picked at random. It is from Jacques F. Houis d'Ormont, of Phoenix, Arizona.

Upon receipt of TD, I started experiments immediately. The explanations concerning the validity of numbers by themselves make sense to me, actually better sense than mechanistic mathematics. I have been very much inter-ested, for instance, in the fact that, in your system, number 9 expresses a circle, or cycle, knowing that the esoteric meaning in pictorial symbolism for the circle is 9, and vice versa. But I have always taken this type of symbolism somewhat like a chemical equation as there is usually a wide gap between theory and practice. But also I like to be honest in attempting an experiment. I soon found out that the THOUGHT DIAL *works*.

"I first tried out very unimportant questions, but which I could check immediately — and it worked. I also found out about the 'psychology' of TD. It always answers your *real* question, not the ones you have sometimes phrased wrong; in other words, the TD, to me, definitely connects your own mind with the mind of the universe, even over-passing, in some instances, your own wording. When the question is clear and direct in your own mind, and when you actually hold a picture of it, TD does work... like *magic*. It works like magic to the extent of again, and over again, giving the same answer to the same question. Having found this out, and having obtained the 'feel' of the TD, I have embarked on questions that were really of interest to me..."

The communications concerning success continue to arrive. From Manhattan Beach, California, Mrs. Paul Bruchez writes: "I purchased the THOUGHT DIAL a short time ago and I find it comes up with some amazingly accurate answers."

We could go on with the communications. From South Daytona, Florida, S. J. Seitz informs us: "We purchased THOUGHT DIAL about two years ago and have had a lot of interesting experiments with it, not to mention a lot of fun and laughs — especially at the way things turned out sometimes. We think the book is great!"

From a medical doctor in New York, who is a psychiatrist, this report: "I purchased a copy of the first edition of TD years ago... and found it extremely interesting. I will agree... that relaxation is a pre-requisite for good results. I am hoping sometime to make a summary of my experiences with THOUGHT DIAL. And I might tell you now that I got the daily double at the race course on one occasion with it."

Let us hope the good doctor soon, in the face of academic prejudice, will publish his findings. We will all be interested.

What have we found out in the years covering the publishing of five editions? Mainly, that the LOCATING LOST ARTICLES section is of tremendous value. Why? Because it "works." Naturally this makes it valuable. But *why* does it work? Here I cannot say with certainty. We have, in TD, uncovered a principle. But, like electricity and magnetism, we have something we can utilize without knowing all the answers to *why*.

We have discovered that the section, PICKING WINNERS, is better for picking winners than is the section, SOUND AND COLOR. I don't know why. But I can "guess." The PICKING WINNERS section adheres closely to known experiments and results . . . and enables the subconscious to "break loose" and express itself freely. The SOUND AND COLOR is arbitrary and does not, it seems to me, allow as much freedom for the subconscious to strike out and come back with the truth of the matter.

When an individual thinks of a question, and comes up with a total of 3 or 7, the answers seem perhaps more definite than with other numbers. *Three is confusion. Seven is something that "comes close" but doesn't quite work out.*

One is the start. Two is the "getting of the second wind."

Four is feeling inhibited. But it is "healthy" in that the native is already perceiving the need for a "breaking away."

Five is analyzing emotional needs. The discovering of love, travel, and adventure.

Six means the native (person asking question) *recognizes that there are domestic conditions which are unsettled. And it is also a crying out for the need to be "understood."*

Eight means the native is concerned about security in connection with the future. How to make more money, more advancement, so the future will be secure. It also tells of a tremendous urge to love and be loved.

Nine means the native realizes, somewhat sadly, that the present situation cannot remain. No status-quo. The end of a cycle. Extra effort must be made toward understanding that certain experiences must now be exchanged for a larger view, greater maturity.

Eleven means the native requires group study. The native must write, teach, share knowledge.

Twenty-two (expressed by the subject in thinking of a question) *tells us he is ready to tear down in order to rebuild . . . his life, career, emotional relationships. He needs incentive to make the move. He needs courage and inspiration. By understanding this through TD, he may be able to see his way clear to take the first and most important step.*

What we are saying, what we have always maintained in these various editions of TD, is that the subconscious *speaks* clearly through numbers. Let us listen!

*   *   *

There are so many letters telling of good to excellent results, of suggestions for experiments, that it might indeed be best to publish these as a special THOUGHT DIAL SUPPLEMENT.

Yet, I do not like, at this moment, to say "goodbye" as far as this, the newest edition of TD is concerned. There is a reason. It is because I want to put across the idea, once again, that we are not dealing with a "game." We have uncovered a dynamic principle: the fact that the mind, like everything else in nature, is willing and able to communicate by way of *numbers.*

If this is so, perhaps we — one day — can reverse the procedure. Perhaps we are on the way to a kind of *Time Machine.*

Here is what I'm getting at. Under hypnosis (let us say for the sake of example), the subject could be given numbers totaling 5. Or could simply be told 5. Then we might expect the subject to respond, while under hypnosis, about areas of his life covered by this numerical (universal) symbol. He is "put in the mood," in other words, by the actual number. Instead of expressing his subconscious through number — he is *given the suggestion of what to express* by the number or series of numbers *implanted* in his subconscious. If "it" works one way, why not see if it works the other way: vice versa?

I would very much like to see a trained psychologist experiment along these lines.

About the "Time Machine." Is it possible that, using our actual THOUGHT DIAL, *we could dial the kind of time we desire?*

Let me explain. The dial is at hand. We wish, let us say, "a romantic evening." We set the dial on 5 and leave it there. Would this aid in producing the desired result? Why not experiment and find out!

A salesman is going out to make a big impression and a big sale. Why not set and keep the dial on number 8? Is it possible that this would "create" an aura (a time, a psychological "push" in the right direction) of commerce, business, achievement, enhanced business, professional standing? Perhaps!

A hostess is to have a party and wants everyone to be "light-hearted." Why not set the dial on 3?

An advertising agency wants to run ads which stress the institutional, humanitarian values of the product or company. Why not (in some subliminal manner) have the figure 9 showing or visible in some inconspicuous corner of the advertisement?

Another type of campaign wants to stress excitement, originality. Then, naturally, we would want the number 1 to be visible somewhere in the illustration.

Can you see the exciting possibilities? The horizons are far-reaching.

We have, in THOUGHT DIAL, actually tapped open a pipeline not only to the individual subconscious, but perhaps we have tapped a treasure-vein which encompasses the "universal mind."

I am going to do more thinking and experimenting along these lines.

Please join me!   Sydney Omarr
                                   September, 1962
                                   Los Angeles, Calif.

172

MELVIN POWERS SELF-IMPROVEMENT LIBRARY

ASTROLOGY

____ ASTROLOGY: HOW TO CHART YOUR HOROSCOPE *Max Heindel*	3.00
____ ASTROLOGY: YOUR PERSONAL SUN-SIGN GUIDE *Beatrice Ryder*	3.00
____ ASTROLOGY FOR EVERYDAY LIVING *Janet Harris*	2.00
____ ASTROLOGY MADE EASY *Astarte*	3.00
____ ASTROLOGY MADE PRACTICAL *Alexandra Kayhle*	3.00
____ ASTROLOGY, ROMANCE, YOU AND THE STARS *Anthony Norvell*	4.00
____ MY WORLD OF ASTROLOGY *Sydney Omarr*	5.00
____ THOUGHT DIAL *Sidney Omarr*	4.00
____ WHAT THE STARS REVEAL ABOUT THE MEN IN YOUR LIFE *Thelma White*	3.00

BUSINESS, STUDY & REFERENCE

____ CONVERSATION MADE EASY *Elliot Russell*	3.00
____ EXAM SECRET *Dennis B. Jackson*	3.00
____ FIX-IT BOOK *Arthur Symons*	2.00
____ HOW TO DEVELOP A BETTER SPEAKING VOICE *M. Hellier*	3.00
____ HOW TO MAKE A FORTUNE IN REAL ESTATE *Albert Winnikoff*	4.00
____ INCREASE YOUR LEARNING POWER *Geoffrey A. Dudley*	3.00
____ MAGIC OF NUMBERS *Robert Tocquet*	2.00
____ PRACTICAL GUIDE TO BETTER CONCENTRATION *Melvin Powers*	3.00
____ PRACTICAL GUIDE TO PUBLIC SPEAKING *Maurice Forley*	5.00
____ 7 DAYS TO FASTER READING *William S. Schaill*	3.00
____ SONGWRITERS' RHYMING DICTIONARY *Jane Shaw Whitfield*	5.00
____ SPELLING MADE EASY *Lester D. Basch & Dr. Milton Finkelstein*	3.00
____ STUDENT'S GUIDE TO BETTER GRADES *J. A. Rickard*	3.00
____ TEST YOURSELF—Find Your Hidden Talent *Jack Shafer*	3.00
____ YOUR WILL & WHAT TO DO ABOUT IT *Attorney Samuel G. Kling*	4.00

CALLIGRAPHY

____ ADVANCED CALLIGRAPHY *Katherine Jeffares*	7.00
____ CALLIGRAPHER'S REFERENCE BOOK *Anne Leptich & Jacque Evans*	7.00
____ CALLIGRAPHY—The Art of Beautiful Writing *Katherine Jeffares*	7.00
____ CALLIGRAPHY FOR FUN & PROFIT *Anne Leptich & Jacque Evans*	7.00
____ CALLIGRAPHY MADE EASY *Tina Serafini*	7.00

COOKERY & HERBS

____ CULPEPER'S HERBAL REMEDIES *Dr. Nicholas Culpeper*	3.00
____ FAST GOURMET COOKBOOK *Poppy Cannon*	2.50
____ GINSENG The Myth & The Truth *Joseph P. Hou*	3.00
____ HEALING POWER OF HERBS *May Bethel*	4.00
____ HEALING POWER OF NATURAL FOODS *May Bethel*	4.00
____ HERB HANDBOOK *Dawn MacLeod*	3.00
____ HERBS FOR COOKING AND HEALING *Dr. Donald Law*	2.00
____ HERBS FOR HEALTH—How to Grow & Use Them *Louise Evans Doole*	3.00
____ HOME GARDEN COOKBOOK—Delicious Natural Food Recipes *Ken Kraft*	3.00
____ MEDICAL HERBALIST *edited by Dr. J. R. Yemm*	3.00
____ NATURAL FOOD COOKBOOK *Dr. Harry C. Bond*	3.00
____ NATURE'S MEDICINES *Richard Lucas*	3.00
____ VEGETABLE GARDENING FOR BEGINNERS *Hugh Wiberg*	2.00
____ VEGETABLES FOR TODAY'S GARDENS *R. Milton Carleton*	2.00
____ VEGETARIAN COOKERY *Janet Walker*	4.00
____ VEGETARIAN COOKING MADE EASY & DELECTABLE *Veronica Vezza*	3.00
____ VEGETARIAN DELIGHTS—A Happy Cookbook for Health *K. R. Mehta*	2.00
____ VEGETARIAN GOURMET COOKBOOK *Joyce McKinnel*	3.00

GAMBLING & POKER

____ ADVANCED POKER STRATEGY & WINNING PLAY *A. D. Livingston*	5.00
____ HOW NOT TO LOSE AT POKER *Jeffrey Lloyd Castle*	3.00
____ HOW TO WIN AT DICE GAMES *Skip Frey*	3.00
____ HOW TO WIN AT POKER *Terence Reese & Anthony T. Watkins*	3.00
____ SECRETS OF WINNING POKER *George S. Coffin*	3.00
____ WINNING AT CRAPS *Dr. Lloyd T. Commins*	3.00
____ WINNING AT GIN *Chester Wander & Cy Rice*	3.00
____ WINNING AT POKER—An Expert's Guide *John Archer*	3.00

____ WINNING AT 21—An Expert's Guide *John Archer*		5.00
____ WINNING POKER SYSTEMS *Norman Zadeh*		3.00

HEALTH

____ BEE POLLEN *Lynda Lyngheim & Jack Scagnetti*		3.00
____ DR. LINDNER'S SPECIAL WEIGHT CONTROL METHOD *P. G. Lindner, M.D.*		2.00
____ HELP YOURSELF TO BETTER SIGHT *Margaret Darst Corbett*		3.00
____ HOW TO IMPROVE YOUR VISION *Dr. Robert A. Kraskin*		3.00
____ HOW YOU CAN STOP SMOKING PERMANENTLY *Ernest Caldwell*		3.00
____ MIND OVER PLATTER *Peter G. Lindner, M.D.*		3.00
____ NATURE'S WAY TO NUTRITION & VIBRANT HEALTH *Robert J. Scrutton*		3.00
____ NEW CARBOHYDRATE DIET COUNTER *Patti Lopez-Pereira*		1.50
____ QUICK & EASY EXERCISES FOR FACIAL BEAUTY *Judy Smith-deal*		2.00
____ QUICK & EASY EXERCISES FOR FIGURE BEAUTY *Judy Smith-deal*		2.00
____ REFLEXOLOGY *Dr. Maybelle Segal*		3.00
____ REFLEXOLOGY FOR GOOD HEALTH *Anna Kaye & Don C. Matchan*		3.00
____ YOU CAN LEARN TO RELAX *Dr. Samuel Gutwirth*		3.00
____ YOUR ALLERGY—What To Do About It *Allan Knight, M.D.*		3.00

HORSE PLAYERS' WINNING GUIDES

____ BETTING HORSES TO WIN *Les Conklin*		3.00
____ ELIMINATE THE LOSERS *Bob McKnight*		3.00
____ HOW TO PICK WINNING HORSES *Bob McKnight*		3.00
____ HOW TO WIN AT THE RACES *Sam (The Genius) Lewin*		5.00
____ HOW YOU CAN BEAT THE RACES *Jack Kavanagh*		5.00
____ MAKING MONEY AT THE RACES *David Barr*		3.00
____ PAYDAY AT THE RACES *Les Conklin*		3.00
____ SMART HANDICAPPING MADE EASY *William Bauman*		3.00
____ SUCCESS AT THE HARNESS RACES *Barry Meadow*		3.00
____ WINNING AT THE HARNESS RACES—An Expert's Guide *Nick Cammarano*		3.00

HYPNOTISM

____ ADVANCED TECHNIQUES OF HYPNOSIS *Melvin Powers*		2.00
____ BRAINWASHING AND THE CULTS *Paul A. Verdier, Ph.D.*		3.00
____ CHILDBIRTH WITH HYPNOSIS *William S. Kroger, M.D.*		5.00
____ HOW TO SOLVE Your Sex Problems with Self-Hypnosis *Frank S. Caprio, M.D.*		5.00
____ HOW TO STOP SMOKING THRU SELF-HYPNOSIS *Leslie M. LeCron*		3.00
____ HOW TO USE AUTO-SUGGESTION EFFECTIVELY *John Duckworth*		3.00
____ HOW YOU CAN BOWL BETTER USING SELF-HYPNOSIS *Jack Heise*		3.00
____ HOW YOU CAN PLAY BETTER GOLF USING SELF-HYPNOSIS *Jack Heise*		3.00
____ HYPNOSIS AND SELF-HYPNOSIS *Bernard Hollander, M.D.*		3.00
____ HYPNOTISM *(Originally published in 1893)* *Carl Sextus*		5.00
____ HYPNOTISM & PSYCHIC PHENOMENA *Simeon Edmunds*		4.00
____ HYPNOTISM MADE EASY *Dr. Ralph Winn*		3.00
____ HYPNOTISM MADE PRACTICAL *Louis Orton*		3.00
____ HYPNOTISM REVEALED *Melvin Powers*		2.00
____ HYPNOTISM TODAY *Leslie LeCron and Jean Bordeaux, Ph.D.*		5.00
____ MODERN HYPNOSIS *Lesley Kuhn & Salvatore Russo, Ph.D.*		5.00
____ NEW CONCEPTS OF HYPNOSIS *Bernard C. Gindes, M.D.*		5.00
____ NEW SELF-HYPNOSIS *Paul Adams*		4.00
____ POST-HYPNOTIC INSTRUCTIONS—Suggestions for Therapy *Arnold Furst*		3.00
____ PRACTICAL GUIDE TO SELF-HYPNOSIS *Melvin Powers*		3.00
____ PRACTICAL HYPNOTISM *Philip Magonet, M.D.*		3.00
____ SECRETS OF HYPNOTISM *S. J. Van Pelt, M.D.*		5.00
____ SELF-HYPNOSIS A Conditioned-Response Technique *Laurence Sparks*		5.00
____ SELF-HYPNOSIS Its Theory, Technique & Application *Melvin Powers*		3.00
____ THERAPY THROUGH HYPNOSIS *edited by Raphael H. Rhodes*		4.00

JUST FOR WOMEN

____ COSMOPOLITAN'S GUIDE TO MARVELOUS MEN Fwd. by *Helen Gurley Brown*		3.00
____ COSMOPOLITAN'S HANG-UP HANDBOOK Foreword by *Helen Gurley Brown*		4.00
____ COSMOPOLITAN'S LOVE BOOK—A Guide to Ecstasy in Bed		4.00
____ COSMOPOLITAN'S NEW ETIQUETTE GUIDE Fwd. by *Helen Gurley Brown*		4.00
____ I AM A COMPLEAT WOMAN *Doris Hagopian & Karen O'Connor Sweeney*		3.00
____ JUST FOR WOMEN—A Guide to the Female Body *Richard E. Sand, M.D.*		5.00

_____ NEW APPROACHES TO SEX IN MARRIAGE *John E. Eichenlaub, M.D.* 3.00
_____ SEXUALLY ADEQUATE FEMALE *Frank S. Caprio, M.D.* 3.00
_____ SEXUALLY FULFILLED WOMAN *Dr. Rachel Copelan* 5.00
_____ YOUR FIRST YEAR OF MARRIAGE *Dr. Tom McGinnis* 3.00

MARRIAGE, SEX & PARENTHOOD
_____ ABILITY TO LOVE *Dr. Allan Fromme* 5.00
_____ ENCYCLOPEDIA OF MODERN SEX & LOVE TECHNIQUES *Macandrew* 5.00
_____ GUIDE TO SUCCESSFUL MARRIAGE *Drs. Albert Ellis & Robert Harper* 5.00
_____ HOW TO RAISE AN EMOTIONALLY HEALTHY, HAPPY CHILD *A. Ellis* 4.00
_____ SEX WITHOUT GUILT *Albert Ellis, Ph.D.* 5.00
_____ SEXUALLY ADEQUATE MALE *Frank S. Caprio, M.D.* 3.00
_____ SEXUALLY FULFILLED MAN *Dr. Rachel Copelan* 5.00

METAPHYSICS & OCCULT
_____ BOOK OF TALISMANS, AMULETS & ZODIACAL GEMS *William Pavitt* 5.00
_____ CONCENTRATION—A Guide to Mental Mastery *Mouni Sadhu* 4.00
_____ CRITIQUES OF GOD *Edited by Peter Angeles* ` 7.00
_____ EXTRA-TERRESTRIAL INTELLIGENCE—The First Encounter 6.00
_____ FORTUNE TELLING WITH CARDS *P. Foli* 3.00
_____ HANDWRITING ANALYSIS MADE EASY *John Marley* 4.00
_____ HANDWRITING TELLS *Nadya Olyanova* 5.00
_____ HOW TO INTERPRET DREAMS, OMENS & FORTUNE TELLING SIGNS *Gettings* 3.00
_____ HOW TO UNDERSTAND YOUR DREAMS *Geoffrey A. Dudley* 3.00
_____ ILLUSTRATED YOGA *William Zorn* 3.00
_____ IN DAYS OF GREAT PEACE *Mouni Sadhu* 3.00
_____ LSD—THE AGE OF MIND *Bernard Roseman* 2.00
_____ MAGICIAN—His Training and Work *W. E. Butler* 3.00
_____ MEDITATION *Mouni Sadhu* 5.00
_____ MODERN NUMEROLOGY *Morris C. Goodman* 3.00
_____ NUMEROLOGY—ITS FACTS AND SECRETS *Ariel Yvon Taylor* 3.00
_____ NUMEROLOGY MADE EASY *W. Mykian* 3.00
_____ PALMISTRY MADE EASY *Fred Gettings* 3.00
_____ PALMISTRY MADE PRACTICAL *Elizabeth Daniels Squire* 4.00
_____ PALMISTRY SECRETS REVEALED *Henry Frith* 3.00
_____ PROPHECY IN OUR TIME *Martin Ebon* 2.50
_____ PSYCHOLOGY OF HANDWRITING *Nadya Olyanova* 5.00
_____ SUPERSTITION—Are You Superstitious? *Eric Maple* 2.00
_____ TAROT *Mouni Sadhu* 6.00
_____ TAROT OF THE BOHEMIANS *Papus* 5.00
_____ WAYS TO SELF-REALIZATION *Mouni Sadhu* 3.00
_____ WHAT YOUR HANDWRITING REVEALS *Albert E. Hughes* 3.00
_____ WITCHCRAFT, MAGIC & OCCULTISM—A Fascinating History *W. B. Crow* 5.00
_____ WITCHCRAFT—THE SIXTH SENSE *Justine Glass* 5.00
_____ WORLD OF PSYCHIC RESEARCH *Hereward Carrington* 2.00

SELF-HELP & INSPIRATIONAL
_____ DAILY POWER FOR JOYFUL LIVING *Dr. Donald Curtis* 5.00
_____ DYNAMIC THINKING *Melvin Powers* 2.00
_____ EXUBERANCE—Your Guide to Happiness & Fulfillment *Dr. Paul Kurtz* 3.00
_____ GREATEST POWER IN THE UNIVERSE *U. S. Andersen* 5.00
_____ GROW RICH WHILE YOU SLEEP *Ben Sweetland* 3.00
_____ GROWTH THROUGH REASON *Albert Ellis, Ph.D.* 4.00
_____ GUIDE TO DEVELOPING YOUR POTENTIAL *Herbert A. Otto, Ph.D.* 3.00
_____ GUIDE TO LIVING IN BALANCE *Frank S. Caprio, M.D.* 2.00
_____ GUIDE TO PERSONAL HAPPINESS *Albert Ellis, Ph.D. & Irving Becker, Ed. D.* 5.00
_____ HELPING YOURSELF WITH APPLIED PSYCHOLOGY *R. Henderson* 2.00
_____ HELPING YOURSELF WITH PSYCHIATRY *Frank S. Caprio, M.D.* 2.00
_____ HOW TO ATTRACT GOOD LUCK *A. H. Z. Carr* 4.00
_____ HOW TO CONTROL YOUR DESTINY *Norvell* 3.00
_____ HOW TO DEVELOP A WINNING PERSONALITY *Martin Panzer* 5.00
_____ HOW TO DEVELOP AN EXCEPTIONAL MEMORY *Young & Gibson* 4.00
_____ HOW TO LIVE WITH A NEUROTIC *Albert Ellis, Ph. D.* 5.00
_____ HOW TO OVERCOME YOUR FEARS *M. P. Leahy, M.D.* 3.00